THE SPLENDOUR OF
SCOTLAND
H.V. MORTON

THE SPLENDOUR OF
SCOTLAND
H.V. MORTON

DODD, MEAD & CO. NEW YORK

Publisher's Foreword

H. V. Morton's first travel books came out almost half a century ago. As a young reporter he drove his bullnosed Morris to the farthest corners of Britain and Ireland, following no special plan but returning with material for his 'In Search' series. These famous books, starting with *In Search of England* in 1927, have been read and reread by millions of enthusiasts. They appeal to readers of any age, who often retrace Morton's own journeys and write to tell him so.

The reason for this is simple. Travel writing at its best calls for imagination as much as for the writing skill to observe and report. Morton has imagination of two kinds. He can project himself back into history and capture distant events and the actors on stage at a particular place he visits. And when the people he meets are contemporaries, of the twentieth century, he understands them and their work with a sympathy they repay. This is just what we would like to manage on our own travels.

This volume presents selections from H. V. Morton's two books, *In Search of Scotland* and *In Scotland Again*, together with 160 pages of photographs in colour and monochrome. The pictures complement and add to Morton's text.

First published 1977
in United States of America

Based on extracts taken from
In Search of Scotland *and* In Scotland Again

Printed in Great Britain by Hazell Watson & Viney Ltd, Aylesbury, Bucks.

ISBN 0-396-07397-2

CONTENTS

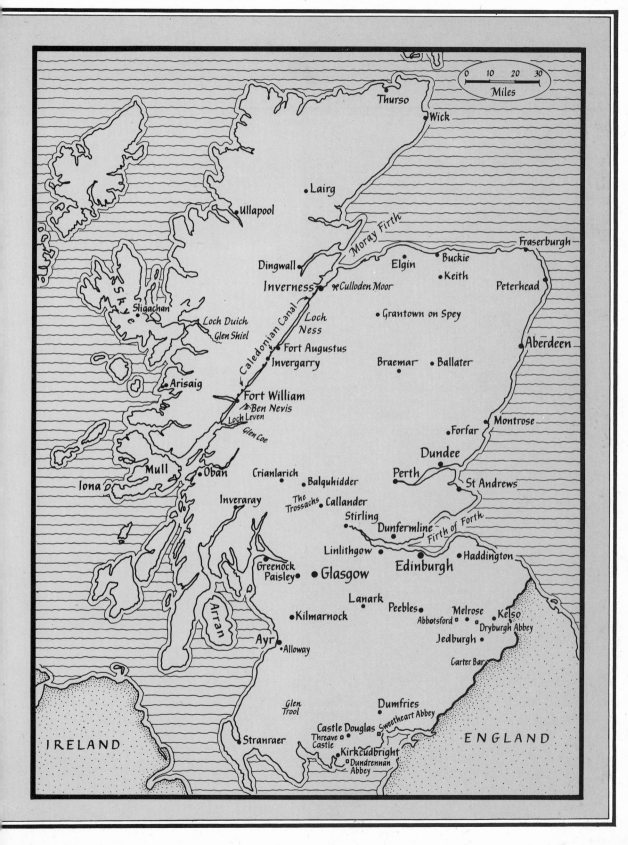

1
The Border
Scott and Abbotsford
Edinburgh

The road, flinging itself round the shoulders of hills, rises and falls, running on in bleak solitude. It narrows to a pass; it opens out into moorland wine-dark with heather; and there is no sound over it but the bleating of sheep and the whistle of wind in the telegraph wires.

The clouds sail in close communion with the hill-crests. Crows like scraps of burnt paper, buffeting the upper air, cry harshly as they are blown downward to a distant valley. Here and there man, exercising his amazing sense of property, has painfully built stone walls, breast-high and brown, to include a few steep acres of tough and soggy grass where black-faced sheep, perpetually optimistic, seek scattered nourishment as they wander, shaggy and unkempt, their long, limp tails swinging in the wind.

This is the Border.

Over it is the loneliness of the sea; the rise and fall of its hills are as the sweep of frozen billows, and the eye, like that of the sailor, searches the solitude for a sign of humanity: a shepherd with his flocks, a farmer in his field, or, best of all, a little white house with a curl of smoke from its chimneys which suggests the presence of the three advance-guards of civilization: a woman, a fire, and children.

As I go on I feel that every bend of the road will bring me face to face with the promised land. A wilderness cannot continue for ever. In the desert you can smell the oasis long before its

Carter Bar

Next page *Melrose Abbey*

palm-trees break the sky-line. So it seems to me
as I mount hills and descend into valleys, cross
streams and skirt the shoulders of hills, that I
can feel Scotland round the next corner. But
how wrong am I! The Border – that No Man's
Land between England and Scotland – is a wide
and persistent wilderness. It has a spirit of its
own. These very rocks thrusting their sharp
jaws from the brown moorland sheltered the
Picts, who sat in the heather listening to the
bees that made their honey-wine as they gazed
southward to the far smoke and the occasional
heliograph of a brazen shield which marked the
western limit of the Roman world. This side of
the Wall was never tamed. It has known many
playmates but no masters. It has made many
songs but no laws.

I stop my car. I take out a map. I climb a stone
wall and strike off over a field to a high waste of
heather; and there I discover my bearings.
What names men have given to these hills!
How snugly they fit! To my left is Corby Pike
and Windy Crag, Dour Hill and Hungry Law;
miles away is Bloodybush Edge and Beefstand
Hill. Six names as right and racy as a ballad!
On my right looms the bulk of Blackman's Law
and beyond it the height of Oh Me Edge. It is
almost too good to be true! What, I wonder, is
the origin of the name of Oh Me Edge? Is it, like
Weary-all Hill, near Glastonbury, a tribute to
the effect of this ridge on the limbs of its victims?

There are certain views in all countries
which must quicken the heart of the man who
sees them again after an absence. Such is the
sight of Scotland from Carter Bar. It is a tender,
lovely view. This is not 'Caledonia stern and
wild'; it is Scotland in a homely, gracious mood
with a smile on her lips, a welcome in her eyes, a
cake on the girdle, a kettle on the hob. It is a
view of Scotland which burnt itself into the
brain of that greatest of all Borderers – Walter

Scott. It would be impossible, I think, for any Scotsman returning home by Carter Bar after years of foreign places to hold back a shout or perhaps a tear. It is so authentically Scotland and could be nowhere else. It seemed to me, as I stood there looking down into the valley, that here is something as definite and unmistakable to a Scotsman as the white cliff of Dover to an Englishman.

The heathery moors slope down to a distant valley. The sun is setting. The sky above the Lammermuirs is red and troubled. The wind drops. The autumn mists far below are creeping from wood to wood. The smoke from chimneys hangs motionless in the air. Thin veils of grey wrap themselves round the foot-hills. Faint white serpents of mist twist above the green-wood, outlining the course of stream and river. It is a study in blue. In the foreground, like a promise of the Highlands, and as notable as a ship at sea, rise the tall peaks of the Eildon Hills, blue as hothouse grapes, standing with their feet among the woodlands of the Tweed. To the far sky lie hills, always hills, fading in graduated subtleties of blue; ahead the long slopes of the Lammermuirs merge westward in the outline of the Moorfoot and the Pentlands. And it is quiet and so still. I can hear a dog barking miles off in the valley.

I am all alone at the Border, one foot in England, the other in Scotland. There is a metal post with 'Scotland' written on it. It is a superfluous post. You do not need to be told that you have come to the end of England. Carter Bar is indeed a gate: the historic barrier between Celt and Saxon; it is the gateway of Scotland.

I sit for a long time watching the light fade from the sky and the mist thickening and the blue deepening. In the hush of evening, with the first star burning above the Eildon Hills, the mystery of the Border winds itself round me like a spell. How can I describe the strange knowingness of the Border? Its uncanny watchfulness. Its queer trick of seeming still to listen and to wait. I feel that invisible things are watching. A blown tree against the sky looks like a crouching man. Out of the fern silently might ride the Queen of Elfland, just as she came to Thomas of Ercildoune in this very country with 'fifty silver bells and nine' hanging from her horse's mane.

Likelier still, it seems as I look down over the moorland stained with heather like blood, that suddenly this land might leap violently to life in pin-points of fire from tree-top to peel tower, from ridge to ridge, filling the dusk with the sound of swords and the mad gallop of horses and the wild clamour of a border raid – 'A Scott! A Scott!' 'An Armstrong!' 'An Elliot!' – as a dark horde sweeps on under the 'lee licht o' the mune'.

The Border is haunted still. It sleeps, but – with one eye open! And it is growing cold. I dip down into Scotland.

In the dusk of a lane I meet a shepherd with his sheep. A small dog with the expression of a professor of mathematics does all the work. She is a little beauty – white muzzle, white chest, paws, and tail tip, but otherwise as black as night. She never barks like the sheep-dogs of the South Downs. She just cruises noiselessly round the flock with the precision of a presiding deity, and if she wishes to rebuke some woolly laggard she gives him a gentle nip in passing and continues, silent and efficient, on the flanks of the trotting grey wave.

That flock of sheep, that dog, and that bent, sandy-haired shepherd could not happen in an English lane.

'A fine nicht,' he says to me.

'It is that!' I reply.

They press past me, a perfect vignette of the Lowlands, towards the stone village, the little lit windows, the warm smell of home . . .

I go on in the deepening dusk to hilly Jedburgh, where a ruined abbey lifts its broken nave to the stars.

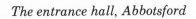
The entrance hall, Abbotsford

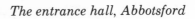

The entrance hall, Abbotsford

In this queer compromise between fairyland and battle-field which is the Border, the lowland abbeys stand with their shattered naves in green grass. Where the Tweed makes wide loops through meadow and woodland the monks, who always recognized a desirable building site, built their churches to the glory of God. Like islands these abbeys rode for centuries above the rough seas of Border battles. They belonged not to Scot or English but to Mother Church – therefore, in a sense, to both of them. Their bells rang out over a land so often scarred by war and pillage; matins and vespers followed one another in calm procession down their chaste aisles, and many an abbot at High Mass must have smelt the pungent incense of Border wrath going up before the high altar with the incense of the Church.

So these abbeys – Kelso, Jedburgh, Dryburgh, and Melrose – as close together as the abbeys of Yorkshire, preached the gospel of love in a land of hate. They were situated gallantly in the front line like four *padres*, helpless to stem the tide of war, nevertheless a comfort to friend and foe.

When you see them one after the other in a day, as I did, you appreciate the horror that must have swept through the Lowlands when men ran panting with the news: 'Melrose is burning! Jedburgh's afire! Kelso's no more!'

It must have seemed the ultimate blasphemy even to a land brought up on curses.

Every unresisting visitor to Scotland finds himself in Abbotsford, the home of Sir Walter Scott, and the scene of the greatest financial drama in the history of literature. Scott found himself at the age of fifty-five faced by a financial crisis which might have driven many a man to suicide. His co-partners failed for £117,000.

'One can imagine the builders scheming and plotting to work in an extra saint or a redundant spiral. There is not an unsculptured inch in the building.'

Ivanhoe. As you skirt the high walls that surround it and observe its towers, its air of having descended from Border keep and baronial castle, it would appear only right that a herald should ride to the sound of trumpets and inquire your status in Debrett. Unfortunately, such thoughts are not of long duration; visitors go in by the tradesman's entrance.

A guide takes you up back stairs to the hall. Here you find yourself in a museum. It is exactly as Scott knew it: an incredibly Gothic apartment, almost as though the novelist had tried to pack the Middle Ages into one room.

He built Abbotsford by instalments. When Washington Irving visited him in 1817 he found him living in a small cottage on the estate, watching the lordly turrets rise up under the hands of workmen. He wrote for ten years to make Abbotsford; and Abbotsford is, I think, one of his finest historical novels. Each new success meant an addition to the house of his dreams, a new room, a new ceiling, a new area of panelling, a few stalls copied from Melrose Abbey or some other extravagant fancy which ministered to his atmosphere.

No man has ever worked with greater intensity to build the perfect home. When the crash came, he looked at the baronial mansion in which he had sunk capital and income, and, with grim pathos, he called it his 'Delilah'.

Scott would rather have been a soldier than a writer. He would rather have been a Border laird than the most famous novelist of his time. The world is full of fine men who succeed in the things that are not those things nearest to their hearts. And Scott was one of them. Fame and money came to him. He used them to make Abbotsford. This house, and the establishment of his family in it, meant more to him than the applause of Europe. He adored the Borderland, and, like a tree, he had to strike his roots down into the very soil of it, or die.

There was no such thing in 1826 as a limited company. Now, Scott was at the height of his powers. He was making from his novels an income of £10,000 a year: and this in the days before film rights and big American royalties.

This middle-aged man decided to devote his life to paying off the debt. It seems as though Fate was determined to test a brain whose fertility can be compared only with that of Shakespeare's. In six years Scott wrote himself into the grave; but in those six years his amazing effort resulted in the payment of £80,000.

The last six years of Walter Scott's life were as heroic as any of the knightly deeds in the pages of his novels.

Abbotsford is a many-turreted mansion standing among trees and built on rising ground which slopes gently to the Tweed. It looks as though it has been composed by the author of

Edinburgh from Calton Hill

When I went to bed in Edinburgh a mighty wind was roaring in the chimney. It was a wind such as I have heard only at sea, howling round a ship, but the gale must have blown itself out in the night. I awakened to a still, autumn morning.

Princes Street has been called the finest street in the kingdom. There are shops on one side only; the other side runs along the edge of a deep ravine, planted with gardens, above which rise the Castle Rock and the high roof-line of Old Edinburgh. On a calm autumn morning the ravine is filled with mist. The shops of Princes Street stand with their doorsteps against a grey wall, dense as the greyness that blows in from the Atlantic at Land's End. If you did not know that there are shops on the north side only, you might be excused the belief that, a landslide having occurred in the night, the south side had fallen into the grey abyss.

It is still and breathless, but overhead is just the faintest smothered flush in the greyness, a promise that the sun will break through in his due time. Then, imperceptibly at first, begins one of the most beautiful atmospheric phenomena in the British Isles. Vague shapes are seen in the mist, or rather you imagine them from a hint here and there of far-off shadows. You realize that something tremendous is hiding there in the immense impenetrability. The mist thins in patches, and again comes that shadow of a shadow, as though some mighty Armada is lying becalmed at anchor in the grey sea.

But the shapes in the mist are not masts and cross-trees. Bit by bit an unbelievable vision uplifts itself, at first like a mirage which hangs uncertain in the air over a desert, and then, etched in toneless grey, as if painted in thin smoke against the sky, a phantom city emerges spire by spire, pinnacle by pinnacle, tower by tower: a ghostly city on the edge of a steep

19

ravine; a Camelot, a Tintagel; a city turreted and loopholed; a city that seems to spring from the mist to the sound of horns; a city that seems still to grasp a sword.

So Old Edinburgh looks down in these autumn mornings over a grey mist, and over many centuries to New Edinburgh.

I had the strangest feeling as I saw this. It was unreal It was ghostly. Round me was New Edinburgh lying on level land, a city of rectangular streets, excessively modern in parts; and in parts as solid and leisurely as a man in a bag-wig leaning on an ebony cane.

Is there another city in the world which marches hand in hand with its past as does Edinburgh; which can look up from its modernity and see itself as it always was, upon a hill intact, impregnable, and still in arms?

I suppose every able-bodied visitor to Edinburgh goes, or is driven by some enthusiastic native, to the top of Arthur's Seat, there to brood like Ashmodeus over the city that lies spread at his feet.

I climbed this hill, and there in the late afternoon recaptured the thrill of early morning. Edinburgh is one of the few cities which cannot be exaggerated. The sun was sinking. Away to the right hand shone the blue Firth of Forth and the 'Kingdom' of Fife; below lay Edinburgh under a blue cap of smoke. From such a height the rocky contour was smoothed out; but how easy to pick out the Castle Rock which brought Edinburgh into being as inevitably as the Thames brought London.

'Why is it called "Auld Reekie"?' I asked a man who shared the hill with me.

'There was a man in Fife yonder–a laird called Durham of Largo,' he replied, 'who regulated evening prayers by the smoke of Edinburgh, which he could see from his own door. When the reek grew heavy as Edinburgh cooked its

supper he used to call his family into the house with: "It's time, noo, bairns, to tak' the buiks and gang to our beds, for yonder's Auld Reekie, I see, putting on her nichtcap!"'

It was not quite prayer time, but the lums were reeking gently, sending up a thin haze of blue, while above it the Castle Rock rose clear and strong in sunlight. I could trace the Royal Mile from the Castle to Holyrood and radiating from it the straggling streets of the old mediaeval town; and northwards of the gap where the railway now runs was New Edinburgh, trim and rectangular, almost American, with Princes Street a long straight line drawn on the edge of a cliff. What a frame for a city! To the south the Pentlands and the Moorfoots; to the east the Lammermuirs and those prominent humps, North Berwick Law and the Bass Rock;

to the north the Kingdom of Fife over the blue water of the Firth, on which many a slow ship steamed towards the clustered roofs of Leith. But look westward, where in graduated blueness are mountains, refined by distance, some the colour of hothouse grapes, some almost mauve, some faint and thin like shadows against the sky: the Highlands! A friendly direction-finder tells me that the king of the western hierarchy is Ben Lomond dreaming above the 'bonny, bonny banks' of his loch.

When darkness comes walk into Old Edinburgh, down the ancient Royal Mile, out of Castle Hill into Lawnmarket, past St. Giles' and into Canongate.

Here are the ghosts of Edinburgh, here in these old stone courtyards, in these dim wynds and closes where pale, significant lamps hang above flights of grey steps, the mighty history of this city stirs a little in its sleep. It is grey, sinister, mediaeval. The harmless figures who lean carelessly at the entry to queer quadrangles, silhouetted against the stairway lamps, seem to be waiting for fellow conspirators, and when they move it seems that they should be easing a dagger in its sheath.

In the stillness of night you stand in Canongate aware of many things: of those ill-fated, sallow Stuarts with their melancholy eyes, of that unhappy, lovely queen who still stirs men's hearts, of John Knox, with his denunciatory finger – a legacy which he has bequeathed to all argumentative Scotsmen – Bothwell, Darnley, and the wild men of that tempestuous court.

The Royal Mile is a mile of memories. There comes a skirl of pipes, a shaggy crowd in torchlight, the glitter of steel, and somewhere in the midst a fair young man on his way to seek a crown . . .

As you go past the dim wynds, peeping here and there, a man with a limp and a fine high brow goes with you. Walter Scott! And it may be, if you are lucky, that you will see Stevenson in a black velvet jacket, bearing an arm-chair on his head to the old infirmary where Henley lies ill.

There are too many ghosts in Old Edinburgh. They crowd round you, pulling at your memory with their eager fingers, trying to drag you into dark, uncomfortable places, attempting to lure you all night long with their story. You must not give way to them as they press round you. So turn about as a bell strikes midnight and bid farewell to the amazing host: to the pale kings and the one dear, misguided queen, to the saints and the sinners, the men of the sword and the men of the pen, and leave them to the old grey courtyards which they knew so well, to the darkness and the stars.

A guide led me to those grim, panelled rooms which give Holyrood its intense sentimental interest, the rooms in which Mary, Queen of Scots, played a little, loved a little, and wept often.

Every visitor to Edinburgh tries to reconstruct the murder of Riccio. The wretched Italian dragged from the skirts of his queen to meet his death is to thousands the most famous scene in Scottish history. It was a horrible deed, but the murder of Riccio was merely 'a stroke in the strife of party, little more reprehensible according to sixteenth-century ethics and practice than a "snap" division might be reckoned in the twentieth century'.

'Aye, it was here that Riccio was supping wi' the queen,' said the guide, 'when a knock came to the door and in walked the murderers . . .'

The room is incredibly small, a mere panelled cupboard. How Mary, Riccio, and the Countess of Argyll managed to dine in comfort there is a mystery. Arthur Erskine, captain of the guard, and Lord Robert Stuart were also in the tiny room on that dreadful March night in 1566.

As the guide talked I tried to get beyond his words to the tragedy of that supper party. Many men have reconstructed the scene, and certainly everyone who visits the room tries to do so. It would have been quiet in Holyrood that night: perhaps a March wind at the windows, and rain. The Earl of Morton had secured all the doors and passages. The conspirators, led by the drunken young king, were creeping towards the little room: Darnley with Ruthven by the narrow, spiral stone stair that opens directly into the supper room; Morton and his band by the main stairs, through the audience chamber and the queen's bedroom.

Darnley was there first, and Ruthven, deadly pale from his recent illness. There would be a second's awful silence while the terrible thing that was to happen took shape. No need for Ruthven's drawn dagger. Riccio's quick brain must have known at once. There would have been questions and the crash of smashed glass as he tried to put the table between himself and the murderers, the falling of candles, and then only one light in the room held by the Countess of Argyll. Things must have happened quickly – the ring of spurs outside as Morton and the other conspirators tramped in; the small room packed with armed men; faces at the doors; angry voices; the young king flinging foul insults at his queen; Riccio's scream of terror and his frantic clinging to her skirts; the wild scramble at the small door as they dragged him out; the struggle with him in the queen's bedroom; the final scuffle in the audience-room beyond as they worried him like hounds; and then the sound of his stabbed corpse bumping from step to step.

Ruthven, who was ill, went back to the small panelled room and asked for a cup of wine . . .

'Years ago,' said the guide, taking me to the audience chamber, 'they used to put raddle down here at the head of the steps and tell people that Riccio's blood would never wash away; but now we have a brass plate.'

Holyrood has fewer brilliant memories than perhaps any palace in the world. I would like to have been there the night that James VI (and the First of England) was surprised by a band of armed men, escaping down the back stairs 'with his breeks in his hand'. James was a welcome touch of comedy to Holyrood. How splendid to

Holyrood: the Supper Room

have seen him, still holding his 'breeks', accepting the repentance of Francis, Earl of Bothwell!

And it must have been a great Saturday night in Holyrood in March 1603 when Sir Robert Carey, who had ridden 400 miles from London in sixty-two hours, came, mud-spattered, demanding an immediate audience with the King of Scotland; and James, again 'breekless', heard that Elizabeth was dead and that he was King of England.

I would like to have been in Holyrood, too, that night in September 1745 when a young man wearing a light-coloured periwig with his own hair combed over the front, a tartan short-coat without the plaid, a blue bonnet, and on his breast the Star of the Order of St. Andrew, rode thoughtfully – the Duke of Perth on his right hand, Lord Elcho on his left – to take possession of Edinburgh in the name of his father, James VIII. The royal salute was a hostile round-shot from the Castle which hit the north-west tower, sending a cloud of plaster and brick down into the courtyard. Bonnie Prince Charlie dismounted while James Hepburn of Keith, who had been 'out' with the 'Old Pretender' in 1715, drew his sword and led the way up the grand staircase. A window opened. Prince Charles Edward – 'Prince of Wales, Regent of Scotland, England, France and the Dominions thereunto belonging' – stood bowing and smiling to the crowds.

On a fine morning if the sun is out it is a good plan to leave Scotland and sit on a wall in Nova Scotia waiting for Edinburgh Castle to open, which happens sharp at 10 a.m. By one of those charming parodies of fact which occur in all old countries the Esplanade – the wide parade ground before the Castle gates – is legally on the other side of the Atlantic. It was declared Nova Scotia territory in the reign of Charles I in order that newly made Nova Scotian baronets might 'take seizin' of their lands! This decree has never been annulled, and is there a lawyer in Edinburgh who will deny the fact that in the eyes of his profession this bit of Scotland is really in Canada?

Edinburgh Castle is more like those up and down fortresses which small boys receive at Christmas than any castle I can call to mind. Its first builders saw a formidable rock rising conveniently up and said:

'Aye, maun, it's a bonny spot for a wee bittie peace!'

Whereupon they climbed up and built a castle which became the despair of their enemies. They tunnelled down like moles, they threw up ramparts, they adapted a crag to civil and military life. Everywhere this rock asserts itself. It springs up into view in the most unlikely places.

Most glorious is the view of Edinburgh from the Argyle Battery. You look over a gorge right down into the distant windows of Princes Street and, beyond, over massed roofs to the blue Firth and the green hills of Fife. High up above Edinburgh is a beautiful Norman chapel. It is one of the smallest churches in Great Britain – only seventeen feet by eleven feet. I suppose an intelligent survey of Edinburgh would start at this small stone church, for it was built to the orders of the Saxon Margaret, wife of Malcolm Canmore, who was driven to the coast of Scotland by a storm four years after William the

Conqueror had invaded England. She was the first and last good gift England was to send to her sister nation for many a long year! As the guide book says, 'She did much to introduce civilization and the beginnings of refinement into Scotland.' Her little chapel has withstood the storms of eight and a half centuries. It is in a sense the real germ of Edinburgh. It was Margaret who persuaded the King to move his capital from Dunfermline, and we may imagine that the pious lady signalled her arrival by founding this small sanctuary. Below it on the ridge Edinburgh must have grown almost at once, for do we not read that good Queen Margaret fed 300 beggars daily?

I wandered away round the ramparts, heard them discharge the gun that startles a stranger in Edinburgh at 1 p.m., and found myself in what is perhaps the most generally interesting room in the Castle. It was here, as an intelligent guide in uniform will tell you in the crisp phrases of an old soldier, that Mary, Queen of Scots, gave birth to the son who became James I of England and VI of Scotland. It is a small room. There is hardly space in it for a four-poster bed. It is almost as small as her supper-room in Holyrood. And the window of this room looks down the face of the cliff to the distant earth. The guide will repeat the traditional story that the infant was let down in a basket from this dizzy window in order that he might be christened in the Catholic faith. I wonder if this is not a confused memory of the removal of the infant James II of .Scotland from the custody of the Chancellor Crichton?

'I assure you the voice of this one man, John Knox, is able in one hour to put more life in us than five hundred trumpets continually bluster-ing in our ears.' Thomas Randolph, the English Ambassador to Scotland, wrote these words in the year 1561 to Sir William Cecil (afterwards Lord Burghley), Queen Elizabeth's chief Secretary of State.

John Knox and Mary, Queen of Scots, are Edinburgh's most famous ghosts. The least imaginative visitor to the city must take away with him the mental picture of stern, fearless Master Knox, on fire with his Calvinism, expounding the broad basis of Scottish Protestantism to the indignant young Catholic queen. The memory of Knox broods over the Canongate. You cannot take a walk past St. Giles' at night without meeting, in imagination, that wizard-like man, severe of face, sallow, long-nosed, full-lipped, his black beard threaded with grey and fully a span and a half in length, his keen blue-grey eyes, heavy lidded, burning beneath a rather narrow brow and under a black velvet bonnet. Or you may visualize him during that surprising but successful domestic experiment, his second marriage at the age of fifty-nine to seventeen-year-old Margaret Stewart, riding home up Canongate with his bride, mounted on a trim gelding and followed by a great crowd. There was nothing of the priest or prophet in his bearing at that moment. He had rather the air of a princeling. His 'bands of taffetie' were fastened with golden rings and precious stones.

Edinburgh has made up for its neglect of Knox's grave by devoting much interest and argument to the marvellous old house in Canongate, approached by an outside flight of steps, called fore-stairs. Tradition claims this house as John Knox's manse, but up-to-date critics appear to agree that it was merely the lodging to which he came to live, broken down in health, for those last two or three years before his end.

It is not known, and will probably never be

known, whether he preached to the crowds from the projecting window or whether he was sitting in this house when a musket shot missed him and lodged in the candlestick which is now, I believe, in Perth Museum. There seems no doubt, however, that in this house were acted the final scenes of his life.

It was from this house that James Melville used to see him led, a feeble old man, walking slowly 'with a furring of martricks about his neck', a staff in one hand, and his secretary, Richard Bannatyne, supporting him under the left arm. He had to be lifted into the pulpit, where he leant exhausted for some time until his spirit conquered his infirmity. Then, as Melville has said so vividly, 'Ere he had done with his sermon, he was so active and vigorous that he was like to ding that pulpit in blads and flee out of it!'

How many Englishmen can translate 'ding that pulpit in blads'? This phrase defeated a French translator of Melville who, having no Scotsman to help him, rendered it as 'he broke his pulpit and jumped into the midst of his auditors'. The words mean that he seemed about to 'break his pulpit in pieces'.

I got into Haddington in the dark and went straight to bed. The bed was a great catafalque with a claret-coloured awning above it. In the morning the girl brought in tea and said:

'And did ye sleep sound?'

'I did. Why?'

'Yon's Thomas Carlyle's bed,' she said. 'The Americans come from far and near to sleep in it.'

What astounding things Americans do! I had an absurd vision of a man in horn glasses reading *Heroes and Hero Worship* and trying to keep awake. Yet it is an interesting bed, for to it the 'Sage of Chelsea' took a love-stricken brain: he slept in it when he was courting pretty Jane Welsh who lived in the main street.

It was seven a.m. I looked with some curiosity out of the window. Haddington is one of the best tonics I can prescribe in a world that seems none too sure of itself. Nothing could look more permanent than Haddington. Its wide, long main street with its worsted-grey houses is built for eternity.

Outside each house or shop a dustbin stood on the pavement's edge. A black-and-white collie with an old man in remote attendance took a flock of sheep up the street. The morning sun fell over the house-tops. The stern stone houses stood with shuttered windows as if closing their eyes to the regrettable sight of dustbins.

It was just the sort of place in which Carlyle would make love.

There can be no other town in Scotland of this size which can claim a longer or a more varied role of fame. John Knox was born here. So was Jane Welsh. So was Samuel Smiles, the author of *Self Help*; and John Brown, the famous divine, although not a native of Haddington, spent all his life here.

Stirling: Cowane's Hospital

2
Stirling
⚜
Aberdeen
⚜
Inverness

The Palace of Linlithgow, like Kenilworth, in Warwickshire, is the roofless shell of its former self, but enough of it remains for a man to prowl round in silence, hearing in imagination the creak of harness, the skirl of pipes, and the uneasy footfall of sad kings and even less happy queens.

In the great dining-hall, with its tremendous fire-place and its gallery, it is possible to reconstruct the banquets held between successive tragedies – the brief moments of music and laughter stolen from fate – and to see those pale, heavy-lidded Stuarts, melancholy, sensuous, piling up an inheritance of intrigue which was to flower in a woman; and all the time sure of nothing in life but failure, until in the decency of time the red hat of Henry, Cardinal Duke of York, came down to extinguish for ever the worn-out flame of their ambition.

It is strange how the tears of women work their way into the stone of buildings. As I sit in these roofless apartments of this old royal palace of Scotland, refurnishing them, hanging tapestries on the walls, strewing rushes and sweet herbs on the floors, I see kings, it is true, but more vivid are their queens. There is a little turret at the end of a long spiral stair that overlooks a lake that lies 150 feet above sea level, and here it was that Margaret, the Queen of James IV, 'all lonely sat and wept the weary hour', waiting day after day for the return of her husband from Flodden – one of the blackest tragedies in Scotland's history.

James IV, twelve Scottish earls, thirteen lords, five eldest sons of peers, fifty chief knights, and 10,000 men fell at Flodden. It often happens when the king or a great hero is cut down in a calamitous battle that popular legend persists in the theory that he left the field in disguise and is still alive. The legend that Lord Kitchener

was not drowned in the *Hampshire* is a modern instance of this. It was so at Flodden; and rather strangely in face of such definite evidence of James's death.

In another part of the palace is the room in which Mary, Queen of Scots, was born. Here is more sorrow. It is a roofless chamber, and through the tracery of the window I can see the great fountain in the courtyard below and the Gothic gateway under which the sad history of Scotland flowed century after century.

I am sure it was a wild December night when the girl who should have been a boy came into the world, with death stalking the Border and the Scots flying from Solway Moss. Tragedy walked side by side with her from the first moment of her life. And the messenger rode north with the unwelcome news to Falkland, where her father, James V, had dragged his broken heart. It was one of Scotland's many wild nights. The English were over the Border. The reivers were out in the dark. The very grass smelt of blood. Eyes were fixed to the bowslits of peel towers from Berwick to Ayr, horsemen came through the night, cattle before them, death behind them, and in the wind that always howls through the soggy heather someone with the 'second sight' must have recognized the spirit of evil.

When they told the King that his child was a lass he said: 'The devil take it,' and died in a few days of a broken heart, they say, certainly of failure, at the age of thirty. In this room in Linlithgow the widowed Queen, holding at her breast the most luckless child in history, lay 'in great fear through divers factions among the principal noblemen . . . contending among themselves for the government of the realm and the keeping of the Princess's person.'

So the dark forces of jealousy and ambition which were to lead her in time to Fotheringay gathered round five-days-old Mary Stuart.

I paused on a hill and looked down on the plain of Stirling. It was early evening and the mists were rising. The rock on which the Castle stands was blue-black against the grey of the fields, the mightiest thing in the wide plain, vast as a galleon on a quiet sea, fretting the sky with the line of its ramparts.

It may have been my mood, it may have been the light that evening, or it may have been something of both, but I went on with the feeling that I was approaching Camelot. Durham is a great city to approach; so is York, whose twin towers beckon you on from Beverley, but Stirling in the evening, with a blown-out storm in the sky and the air drenched with the melancholy of autumn, is like a chapter of Malory. Your heart goes out to it; something of the good manners of an age of swords seems to meet you half-way and lead you on to the grey battlements.

Once in Stirling these expectations are not realized. Where would they be? Stirling has streets like other towns, suburbs, and neat houses, shops of all kinds which prove to you, in spite of all appearances to the contrary, that it does indeed belong very much to the world.

Stirling is the twin brother of Edinburgh. I am sure that every writer on Scotland has already called this town the 'sister' of Edinburgh; but I cannot feminize these grizzled old sinners who sit up on their hills like robber barons with swords across their knees. The family resemblance is, however, absurd. Stirling has not grown so great in the world as his brother. Events have not shaped him in the same way. In one thing, however, they are equal: in battle, in the friendship of kings and queens, in experience, and in the rich memories of the past.

Edinburgh is like an old soldier who has entered public life; Stirling is like an old soldier living in a house full of the trophies of his youth, fingering a sword, shaking his head over a battle-axe, sighing mysteriously over a glove, and, though acutely conscious of the present, liable at any moment to withdraw himself into more exciting reverie.

The twin rocks on which the twin castles of Edinburgh and Stirling rise spring from the plain at the same angle. When you see Stirling for the first time, especially in the evening, you feel that you are seeing a vision of Edinburgh as he was in his youth.

And the rock of Stirling, when you stand and look up at it from the flat lands where tournaments were held, or from those meadows still scarred with the ghosts of ancient gardens, is even grander than that of Edinburgh. There must be moments throughout the year, in early morning perhaps, when Scotland can show no prouder sight than Stirling rising from the plain. The view from the ramparts of Stirling Castle can hold its own with any view in this world. A man who travels much sees hundreds of views which impress him, but few which he can never forget. The panorama which lies below Stirling Castle is unforgettable.

Crail, Fifeshire

When the benevolence of the late Andrew Carnegie descended on the world in a shower of organs and free libraries the old town of Dunfermline emerged, slightly dazed, from the peace of centuries to grapple with public swimming-baths, libraries, public parks, colleges of hygiene, and generally to learn the responsibility of having given birth to a millionaire with the strong homing instinct of the Scot.

The experience of Dunfermline is unique. There can be no other spot like it in the world. Here is a great and ancient town, the Winchester of Scotland, which played its part as the capital city before Edinburgh emerged from the mists of history. All its inspiration was in the past. It sat in the 'Kingdom' of Fife at its spinning-loom, rather like the dear old lady, in the Lyceum drama, whose son is lost in foreign parts.

One day, however, he knocks at the cottage door, often on the eve of an eviction order, and, lo! the desert blossoms and the old lady finds herself smothered in expensive affection. It is one of the prettiest stories in the world. *And this has happened to a whole town!*

One of the finest things which Carnegie did for his native town was to give Pittencrieff as a public park. In this lovely glen birds are tamer than I have seen them in any town. Children are encouraged to make pets of them, and of the squirrels which come and shake their tails almost under your feet.

'Ye know the reason why he gave us the glen?' asked a man with whom I was discussing the dollars of Dunfermline. 'Ye see, when the late Mr. Carnegie was a wee lad he wasna pairmitted to enter the park. It was a private property. And he never forgot it! When the time came he gave it to Dunfermline so that no wee child should ever feel locked oot of it as he was. . . . Aye, it was a graund thocht. . . .'

And the other side of Dunfermline? An old grey town with hilly streets and a ripe air of experience; grey ruins; Norman arches; an old abbey whose nave has the finest Norman pillars in Scotland.

Under a memorial brass lies the body of Robert the Bruce. In 1818 they opened the tomb and discovered the great patriot wrapped in a shroud interwoven with threads of gold. Those who looked at his body saw that the ribs were sawn through. Thus the old story was proved true that Bruce's heart was taken from his body after death at his own request and borne on a crusade . . .

Bruce and Andrew Carnegie link up over the misty centuries in the 'auld grey toon' of Dunfermline. One beat the English at Bannockburn; the other beat everybody at Pittsburg, both using the same metal. One the King of Steel; the other the Steel King!

Never shall I forget my first night in St. Andrews. A dangerous small boy was swinging a new driver at an invisible ball on the hotel mat. Three men, leaning on the visitors' book, were arguing about a certain mashie. A girl in the lounge was shrilly defending her conduct on the home green. At the next table to me in the dining-room sat a man in plus-fours who cheered his solitude by practising approach shots with his soup-spoon. When the spoon, fresh from a bunker of oxtail, was no longer playable, he did a little gentle putting with a bread pill and a fork.

The town is a delight; an old grey town of ancient houses and monastic ruins; full of men and women with splendid scarlet gowns; of happy meetings in cakeshops; of wayside gossip; of fine windows full of silk nightdresses, Fair Isle jumpers, brogues, golf clubs, golf bags and, strange to say, one or two bookshops, presumably for the use of the Oxford of Scotland.

All the time the North Sea unwraps itself restlessly on the curve of the lovely bay, beyond which lies that sacred strand, the golf links, backed by the stern bulk of the MCC of golf – the Royal and Ancient.

Had St. Andrews Cathedral not been destroyed, the town might well have been called the Oxford and Canterbury of Scotland. It is the only town in Scotland which is soft and mellow as Oxford is mellow; and the ruined cathedral, although no larger than Chester Cathedral, must have been one of the finest examples of pointed Gothic in Scotland.

Knox, who is usually blamed for inciting the populace to tear down the Popish churches, did, as a matter of fact, on several occasions, attempt to restrain the frenzy let loose by his eloquence. When in 1559 he came to St. Andrews to denounce 'the hellish priests, bellygods and shavelings', his sermons did, it is true, cause the multitude to tear down the images

from the cathedral, but there was no wholesale sabotage. The building is a ruin today because it was allowed to fall into ruin, and once the roof of a large building like a Gothic cathedral is allowed to collapse the end is not far off. Also, the size of the parish church of St. Andrews contributed more to the ruin of the cathedral than even the anger of Knox's followers because, as soon as the priests fled, Protestantism transferred itself to the Town Church and permitted the cathedral to fall slowly into decay.

I went to the Castle of St. Andrews which stands on a jutting cliff above the sea. There is little left of it save a gate-house, a dungeon and a secret passage that must delight the heart of every boy who visits this town.

The guide took me to the 'Bottle Dungeon' – a ghastly *oubliette* shaped rather like a bottle, its only entrance the neck, the body being shaped out of the solid rock. He also took me to the gate-house and told me how in March 1545 George Wishart, the Protestant reformer and friend of John Knox, was burned to death at a stake in front of the castle, and how Cardinal Beaton, lying at ease on velvet cushions, watched him die. He said that when Wishart had forgiven the executioner he saw Beaton at the window of the tower and prophesied his early death by violence.

Two months after Wishart had been burned, sixteen men who had sworn to be revenged on Beaton gathered at St. Andrews. They entered the castle and murdered the Cardinal.

To the Catholics it was an act of unspeakable horror and sacrilege; to the Protestants of England and Scotland it was a sign of hope and triumph. The castle was besieged for a year. But with the coming of the French there could only be one end – surrender. The gallant outlaws gave in and were bundled into galleys by the French troops and taken to France. Among them was John Knox. For nineteen months the man whose voice was to shake Scotland to her foundations was a slave chained to the bench of a French galley.

On one occasion a ship in which he was slaving came within sight of St. Andrews. A fellow slave asked him if he knew the place. Yes, he replied, it was at St. Andrews that he had preached his first sermon and he did not doubt but that God would preserve him to preach there again.

As soon as St. Andrews castle was captured, the victorious army discovered a gruesome relic in the 'Bottle Dungeon'. The body of His Eminence, Cardinal Beaton, was found preserved in a solution of salt.

Dundee lifted its chimneys in a cloud of smoke. But even as I looked the wild wind that whipped the Tay into white flecks blew the smoke towards the Highlands; and, clear against the hills, I saw the third largest city in Scotland.

There was nothing very 'bonnie' about Dundee from the ferry, except its amazing situation. What a place for a city! Its wharves and docks lie against a two-and-a-quarter-mile wide river, and within sight, almost within sound, of the sea. It is like Liverpool, the Tay its Mersey, and where the river widens is the blue-green line of the ocean.

Dundee was that morning busy with its marmalade, its jute mills, its cakes, its linen. There was a deep Manchester rumble over the stone setts as the jute wagons went by. It is a city that has mysteriously effaced its past. It has a long and exciting history. William Wallace was a grammar-school boy there. In the old days

England took it, and Scotland won it back almost as frequently as Berwick. Even if one did not know these things, such names as Nethergate and Seagate are as good as a pedigree stamped and sealed by the College of Heralds; but, look where you will, Dundee has replaced the ancient by the modern.

The first among Dundee's treasures is the great hill of Dundee Law. Edinburgh and Stirling both have high places from which their citizens may take a broad view of life; but Dundee snuggles against a perfect tower of rock from which a man can look down the very chimneys of the city.

Here is another great view in Scotland, different from anything I have seen, and, in its way, as magnificent. Dundee lies below – street piled on street, chimney above chimney, the broad Tay crossed by the astonishing two-and-a-quarter-mile bridge. To the left the docks and the open sea; right ahead, over hills and remote in distance, the golden sands and the roofs of St. Andrews. On a sunny day, with the wind blowing over Dundee Law, your blood tingles and you want to shout.

But turn round and look inland. There is that promise that gleamed so far off at Stirling; there are the Highlands of Scotland! The Grampians, still remote and still mysterious, blue and cloud-tipped, lie against the sky.

41

I was told that I would not like Perth; but I never pay attention to such prophecies. I found Perth full of atmosphere. I was astonished to learn that Dr. Macfarlane, in his famous *Tour*, considered Perth to be pervaded by 'the cheerful air of a provincial town in England'. This is, to me, incomprehensible. The air is cheerful enough, but it is as Scottish as a plate of cocka-leekie or a warm bannock.

The winds of the Highlands blow into Perth day and night. And the voice of 'Pairth' is the voice of Scotland! Here you meet memories of the clans for the first time. As soon as the stranger begins talking about Perth he is told how the Clan Chattan and the Clan Quhele fought thirty champions a side on the North Inch. Perth like an English provincial town? You might as well put a Highlander in gaiters and call him a Devonshire yokel!

Never for one minute can you feel unconscious of the wildness which lies beyond the gates of Perth: the roads go north to Pitlochry and Drumtochter, to Blairgowrie, and to the Spittal of Glenshee; and at night, as you walk through grey stone streets, modern but still, in their sky-line and their grim bulk, recalling a more ancient Perth, you smell a wind that comes sweet over miles of desolate heather.

If you would see a perfect picture postcard stretch of Scotland take the road from Braemar to Ballater any afternoon when the sun is shining. Every yard of this road is a coloured postcard. All the graciousness, all the gentleness, all the sweetness and the prettiness which is denied the majestic mountain pass from Perth has taken root in the valley of the Dee. Here on fine days the Highlands wear a perpetual smile. It is true that there are wild places, but you are never quite deceived by

Crathes Castle, Aberdeenshire

them: you know that every pine-tree near Balmoral has a valet, and that no matter how cold the wind, how cruel the mountain-side, how bleak the rolling moor, there is a hot bath at the end of every day.

I went on beside the Dee, for this road is like a promenade beside the river, and I saw that characteristic sight, a fisherman up to his thighs in the stream wielding a great salmon-rod, in the background an experienced and slightly cynical ghillie holding an as yet un-necessary gaff. Over the trees on the right of the road fluttered the Royal Standard from a turret of Balmoral. This baronial castle of white Crathie granite lies at the foot of Craig Gowan beside a bend of the Dee, and it is haunted by the ghost of an elderly lady in black who ad-mires the scenery from a little trap drawn by a shaggy Highland pony. The Highlands will never forget Queen Victoria. I talked to an old man in Braemar who referred to her always with a spiritual genuflexion as 'her late gracious majesty'.

Next page *Dunkeld Cathedral*

Aberdeen, or to give it the right sub-title, the City of Bon-Accord, is obviously one of the corner-stones of modern Scotland. Lacking Aberdeen, Scotland would not be so securely balanced. This is a city which, to mix metaphor, nails down the map of Scotland on the north-east with the hard metal of the Scottish character. It is rather curious to discover this vivid and stimulating community in a part of Scotland where you might have expected a kind of haphazard Galway.

Aberdeen impresses the stranger as a city of granite palaces inhabited by people as definite as their building material. Even their prejudices are of the same hard character. The beauty of Aberdeen is the beauty of uniformity and solidity. Nothing so time-defying has been built since the Temple of Karnak. And it is obvious that in a few years when certain ancient streets disappear that Aberdeen will be, after Edinburgh, the most architecturally impressive city in all Scotland.

It is early morning. The sun is rising. The sound of Aberdeen at this time is a bright jingle as dray horses plod steadily over the stone roads. I go through the half light to one of Aberdeen's most fascinating sights – the morning auction in the Fish Market.

At the bottom of Market Street I am pulled up by an unexpected beauty. The rising sun, struggling through a veil of clouds in thin streamers of lemon-yellow and flamingo-pink, flings a bridgehead in dark silhouette against the sky. I have no doubt that in ordinary lights this is a very ordinary bridge, merely a path of steel girders linking quay to quay. But in the early morning its round turrets, like a Border keep, stand mirrored in the still water of a dock looking for all the world like some ancient fortress of romance dreaming above its moat.

The Fish Market is something that no visitor to Aberdeen should miss. Every fish market is

fascinating. That man is not normal who will not linger beside a fisherman in the hope of prying into his basket. How much more exciting, then, are these markets on whose floors are laid out the stranger mysteries of deeper waters?

This fish market is the largest in the country. It is a broad, covered way built right round the Albert Basin. The trawler fleet lies – 'berthed' is, I suppose, the right word, but 'parked' is much more expressive – at the quay-side, thick as motor-cars at the Derby. They steam gently with the effort of their incoming. Their decks are foul with fish-scales and slippery with crushed ice. Salt is on their smokestacks, and their high fo'c'sles are wet still, with North Sea spray. The grimy faces of engineers peer up from hatchways; down companionways clatter the crews in enormous thigh boots. Vivid, arresting, and even, as are all things connected with the sea, exciting as this fleet is, it simply fades before the spectacle of its cargo.

Imagine a million bare babies being soundly smacked, and you have the sound of Aberdeen Fish Market as a million fish are slapped down on the concrete! The sound of this slapping continues perhaps for an hour until each ship has landed her catch. Then come men who sort out the fish according to their kind, and other men who take each limp pyramid and dress it by the right in neat, fearfully defunct, rows. The sight of so much death before breakfast might be considered a saddening experience. The same number of sheep or oxen lying prone would turn any man towards vegetarianism; but death, which is, no doubt, as real to a fish as to a mammal, is to us the normal condition of a fish. Only gold-fish are pathetic in death, and then probably because their end may seem to reflect on us.

I walk, it seems for miles, past dead fish. Imagine the Strand from Temple Bar to Charing Cross carpeted with haddock, plaice, soles, whiting, hake, cod, skate, ling, and lobsters, and you have a hazy idea of the thing that happens in Aberdeen every morning of the year. I am told that things might be better with the trawler trade; but I cannot believe it. This daily harvest of the sea is an amazing spectacle. It is difficult for a landsman to believe that it can go on day after day the year round.

Elgin Cathedral

Elgin has a prosperous, retired-looking air. I feel that its tradesmen specialize in local gentry.

In the days when Scotland was Catholic the great Cathedral of Elgin must have been one of the finest examples of pointed Gothic in the land. Now it is the most picturesque religious ruin north of the Border abbeys. I saw it in hot sunlight, the shadows of its fractured towers lying in broad shadows across the green grass of the nave. The old lady who lives in the gate-house took me round and led me to the graves of the Gordons and into the chapter-house whose piscina is linked with a romantic story enlivened by that financial sequel so dear to the Scottish heart.

When Bonnie Prince Charlie was marching with the clans in 1745 a good-looking girl called Mary Gilzean in the neighbouring parish of Drainie ran away with a soldier called Anderson. They fled across the seas, where the soldier and his delicately brought-up wife lived a life of such tragic privation that it unhinged her mind. She appeared in Elgin three years later carrying an infant son in her arms. She had nowhere to go, but happening to pass through the ruins of Elgin Cathedral she found a resting-place in the chapter-house, cradling her baby in the stone piscina in which, in old times, the priest washed his hands before saying Mass. Apparently the poor woman became a local character. The boy grew up and received lessons in Elgin Grammar School in return for certain menial labours. Eventually he entered the service of the East India Company as a drummer-boy. Long years after his mother's grave had been forgotten he became Lieut.-General Anderson. He died in London in 1824, aged seventy-seven, leaving the sum of £70,000 to found an institute in Elgin for the care of ten old people and the education of 390 children. The moral of work is – education!

The road dips down from Nairn to Moray Firth and Inverness.

I have tried to describe views whose beauty has appealed to me from the Border onward, but this view on a day of brilliant sun is one of the most perfect things I know. There are glimpses through pine woods of distant blue waters. The hills round Moray Firth are that incredible Atlantic blue which almost breaks the heart – the blue of Aran and Achill Island off the west coast of Ireland – a blue so blue, and yet so soft, that to look at it is to think of the islands of the Hesperides or the land of the Lotus Eaters. It is a colour out of this world: it is a paint they use only in heaven. Beyond the Firth lie piled the distant hills of Cromarty and Dornoch, etched in the same even, tender magic; and, more remote still, lying in a haze of heat, are the clustered highlands of Sutherland-shire and the coast-line that swings up to Caithness.

Inverness is unique among the cities of Scotland as York among those of England. It has none of York's visible age, yet, strangely enough, here is a city which has swept away its antiquities without losing an air of antiquity. It is almost as though centuries of history steam upward through the soil of Inverness. Like Edinburgh, Dundee, Stirling and Perth, it has the appearance of having been founded by a member of the Royal Academy in a landscape mood. No human communities, except perhaps the hill towns of Tuscany, are so fortunate as the cities and towns of Scotland in their surroundings. That is the virtue of a turbulent youth. Peaceful and law-abiding countries build their towns in sheltered places; wild countries fly to the protection of hills. Now that the savage seas have ebbed, these cities of Scotland are left like great arks stranded magnificently on their Ararats.

The hill of Tomnahurich, dark with cypress and with cedar of Lebanon, rises above the left bank of the Ness. It is a hill of death. When primeval torrents burst their way to the sea this hill, opposing them, stood firm; and the waters passed on either side of it. The people of Inverness have made of it the most beautiful cemetery in the world.

Some say that Tomnahurich means 'hill of the fairies', others 'hill of the boat'. A Celtic eye is not necessary to see this enormous woody mound as a ship lying keel-up covered with the dark green weeds of the sea. It is, of course, haunted. It knows all about the children which the fairies steal from time to time. You are wise to keep away from it on dark nights, for that is the time when you might hear the thin piping of a fairy reel. Someone would come to invite you to the dance. That is fatal. Everyone in Inverness knows what happened to Farquhar Grant and Thomas Cumming of Strathspey, two street musicians who were persuaded to play reels for a dance held inside Tomnahurich. When the dance was over they came out into Inverness surprised by everything round them. The wooden bridge on which they crossed the Ness was a substantial bridge of stone. People meeting them in the streets jeered at their quaint dress. The fairy dance had lasted a whole century! When the two pipers entered a church they crumbled into dust on hearing the name of the Deity.

One of the world's greatest romances came to grief on Culloden Moor, four miles from Inverness. Is there a more perfect hero than Prince Charles Edward – a more daring tale than that of his attempt to place his father on the throne of the Stuarts? From the moment he landed in Scotland until he escaped, a be-

draggled fugitive, from the mountains of the Hebrides, Bonnie Prince Charlie marches through romance between Don Quixote and d'Artagnan. It is surprising to remember that James Watt was already born. The world was pregnant with the new age. And this young man strides through it sword in hand on the last personal gallantry of kingship . . .

Culloden is the only battle-field in the world which is as the poet or the antiquary would have it. Bannockburn is merely a field; Flodden is smiling cornland; Waterloo is a place of farms; even the Ypres Salient is already obliterated by crops. On Hell Fire Corner now stands a little new house, a line of washing on posts, and chickens busily scratching in the cinders. How swiftly nature covers up the scars of battle! Culloden, alone of all the battle-fields known to me, is still drenched with the melancholy of its association: it is the only battle-field I know which contains the graves of the fallen, buried in trenches as they died.

Small, weather-worn stones rise from the heath and stand among the slim trees. On these stones are written the names of the Highland clans who died for the Stuarts.

I walked over the wet grass and spelt out the names: 'Clans McGillivray, MacLean, Maclachlan, Athol Highlanders.'

That is on one stone. Not far off another bears the words, 'Clan Stewart of Appin'; another, 'Clan Cameron'; a third, 'Clan Mackintosh.'

A little burn flows in a hollow; it hardly deserves the name of burn: it is little more than a sogginess of the grass; but there is a spring near a fence and over this is a stone with these words: 'The Well of the Dead.'

During the action numbers of wounded Highlanders crawled to this spring to slake their thirst, among them a chieftain who was shot as he was raising his head. He fell with his head

in the spring. After the battle the little pool of water was found choked with stiffened corpses, and from that day to this no one will drink from 'The Well of the Dead'.

A few yards farther on, at the edge of a cornfield, is the laconic inscription on a stone:

The Field of the English.
They were buried here.

I remembered, as I looked at this memorial, a strange conversation I once heard in a London club. An Englishman declared that this inscription was the only thing that made his blood boil in all Scotland.

'So curt and unchivalrous!' he cried. 'And they were even growing corn on them; actually making a profit out of them!'

Someone ventured to suggest that chivalry had little part in Culloden.

'Well, anyhow,' he replied, 'that stone makes me mad! I love the Scots, but when I saw that stone I said, "Blast Scotland!" . . .'

I remember wondering who was speaking, because this man's great-grandfather was governor of Fort William! Perhaps he was not responsible for his feelings.

I had no such emotion. It seemed to me a perfectly adequate memorial. There were only fifty English dead at Culloden. From the English point of view it was, as far as casualties went, a mere skirmish; but to the other side it was the Flodden of the Scottish Gael.

One thousand two hundred clansmen lay dead on the moor. This moor is the grave not only of Jacobitism but also of the clan system. The Highlands were never to be the same again. The traditions of centuries lie buried there; but from the green mounds of Culloden was to rise a united Scotland. Charles Edward did not know as he made for the heather that his defeat had brought Highlands and Lowlands together and had welded the Scottish nation.

3
The Highlands

'At the end of the glen near Rhiconich I caught
my breath at the sight of a monster called Arkle,
who stands by himself to the left, towering all
alone, to the height of 2,580 feet, a finely curved
isolated mass rising like a Gibraltar.'

Opposite *Loch Stack and Ben Arkle,
Sutherland*

Below *Duncansby Stacks, near John o'Groats,
Caithness*

Next page *Loch Inchard, Finlochbervie*

Opposite *The Slioch from Glen Grudie, Wester Ross*

Below *The Quinaig and Loch Nedd, Sutherland*

Next page *Ben More Coigach, Ross and Cromarty*

'I came to a lovely village called Tongue, that lies on the shores of the Kyle of Tongue, and here I was in the world of loch and yellow weed, of high, impregnable hill and dark gorge, of brown moor and wild forest.'

Opposite *Ach nan Pulag, Tongue, Sutherland*

Below *Ben Hope and Kyle of Tongue, Sutherland*

Next page *Plockton, Ross and Cromarty*

Ben Loyal and Loch Hacoin

Next page *Loch Morar, Inverness-shire*

'Far ahead I saw a range of hills which seemed to me one of the grandest in the whole of Scotland: Ben Loyal to the left and, flanking him, Ben Hope. What a magnificent contrast these two giants make as they stand side by side: Ben Loyal, the Coolin of Sutherland, rising in a series of precipices to a height of 2,505 feet, to end in a series of shattered crags like the spires of a cathedral; and Ben Hope, a great dome, higher by 500 feet, but smooth and tame.'

The Five Sisters of Kintail, Ross and Cromarty

4
The Road to the Isles
Skye

I left Inverness to follow the Caledonian Canal to Fort Augustus and Fort William, two names which Fenimore Cooper might have written on the map of Scotland. These forts were, of course, built in the eighteenth century to subdue the Highlanders, just as similar forts were built in Canada to subdue the redskins.

I entered a country of glens and bens and sudden bright flashes of lake water. The Canal looks less like a canal than any waterway in the world. It is not actually a canal: it is merely a series of short cuttings which connect four lochs with each other. There are thirty-eight miles of loch and twenty-two miles of canal; and a ship on its way to or from Inverness sails one hundred feet above sea-level when it enters Loch Oich!

What scenery, what primeval wildness, what splendid solitudes, what lonely mountain-crests, what dark gloom of pine and larch, what sudden bright glimpses through trees of deep water reflecting the curves of guardian hills! If I were asked to indicate the most romantic inland voyage in Europe I would vote for the journey up or down the Caledonian Canal. The Rhine cannot hold a candle to it. The sameness of Rhineland hill and castle and scraggy vineyard palls and wearies, except through St. Goar and near Bingen; but the Great Glen through which the Caledonian Canal runs is a luscious extravagance in landscape, rich in its variety, almost terrible in its wild splendour.

It is wrong to motor, as I did, along the Canal. I will some day return and glide the length of it in a steamer.

Loch Morlich, Inverness-shire

The road to Fort Augustus runs for twenty-four miles beside the northern bank of Loch Ness. This is my idea of a perfect Highland loch. It is never greater than a mile in width, so that, unlike some lakes, it cannot pretend to be the sea. Here for twenty-four miles is a changing beauty of hill, woodland, and water. I have never seen inland water which looked deeper: it is actually black with fathoms – 130 fathoms, I am told.

The deepest, most sinister portion of the loch is that opposite the ruined shell of Urquhart Castle. Here the water is 750 feet in depth! And the old castle sits grimly on a bluff overlooking the deep water and sings a song of battle and siege. Weeds grow over it and try to press apart its massive stones, but the old building gazes steadily down to Loch Ness, and Loch Ness gazes back with rarely a ripple on her black face; and it seems to you that both of them have appropriate secrets . . .

It was along this road on an August day in 1773 that the bulky form of Dr. Johnson was observed by the adoring Boswell for the first time on horseback. The Doctor, Bozzy noted,

rode well. It was beside Loch Ness that Johnson had his amusing interview with the Highland woman, old Mrs. Frazer:

'I perceived a little hut,' wrote Boswell in his *Tour to the Hebrides*, 'with an old-looking woman at the door of it. I thought that here might be a scene that would amuse Dr. Johnson, so I mentioned it to him. "Let's go in," said he. We dismounted and we and our guides entered the hut. It was a wretched little hovel of earth only, I think, and for a window had only a small hole, which was stopped by a piece of turf that was taken out occasionally to let in light. In the middle of the room or space which we entered was a fire of peat, the smoke going out at a hole in the roof; she had a pot upon it, with goat's flesh boiling. There was at one end, under the same roof but divided by a kind of partition made of wattles, a pen or fold, in which we saw a good many kids.

'Dr. Johnson was curious to know where she slept. I asked one of the guides, who questioned her in Erse. She answered with a tone of emotion, saying, as he told us, she was afraid we wanted to go to bed with her. This coquetry, or whatever it may be called, of so wretched a being was truly ludicrous. Dr. Johnson and I afterwards were merry upon it. I said it was he who alarmed the poor woman's virtue. "No sir," said he. "She'll say, There came a wicked young fellow, a wild dog, who I believe would have ravished me, had there not been with him a grave old gentleman who repressed him; but when he gets out of sight of his tutor, I'll warrant you he'll spare no woman he meets, young or old." "No, sir," I replied, "She'll say, There was a terrible ruffian who would have forced me had it not been for a civil, decent young man who, I take it, was an angel sent from heaven to protect me."

In such a way did Johnson and Boswell enliven that romantic ride to Fort Augustus.

Loch Garry

If you wish to penetrate a country as wild and desolate as anything in the British Isles, take the road from Fort Augustus that branches right at Invergarry and leads you, in the course of forty miles or so, through Glen Garry into Glen Shiel.

Glen Garry is exquisite. Beyond the still, blue loch the river flows with Highland grace through a valley green with birch trees. Even an unobservant eye will notice the dark clumps of nettles that mark the ruins of old crofts in this sweet glen. They dot the flat lands near the river and they lie like old sores on the hills. These are the remains of houses burnt down or left to rot during the 'Clearances'.

I doubt whether the agrarian history of any country in Europe can match the heartlessness of that time, when Highland families were burned out of their homes and shipped abroad to make way for sheep runs and deer forests. The Clearances were, of course, a result of the '45 Rebellion. As an old Highland chief said in the year 1788: 'I have lived in woeful times. When I was young the only question asked concerning a man of rank was, How many men lived on his estate? Then it was, How many black cattle it could keep? but now it is, How many sheep will it carry?'

The disarming of the clans after the defeat of Prince Charlie, the abolition of feudal power, the sweeping away of hereditary jurisdiction, spelt the death of the old Highland social system. In the old days, when every Highland chief was a little king with his own army, his wealth and pride were naturally in the number of men who would follow him to the cattle-lifting or the clan battle. When Lowland law came into the Highlands and such things were made illegal, the clansman, if not an actual burden on his chief, became a tenant, and the chief himself became a laird.

The road climbed towards Tomdoun; It grew bitterly cold. Down below the clouds moved sluggishly over the hillsides; sometimes they thinned, or the wind blew rifts in them, and I saw a gleam of water where the River Garry ran like a silver thread through the dark valley.

I remembered the story of the last Glengarry, Colonel Alastair Ranaldson MacDonell, who died in 1828. It seems impossible that such a character could have existed in modern times. He was the last Highland chief to travel the country with a band of retainers, known as Glengarry's 'tail'. He seemed quite unconscious of a changed age and lived, dressed, and behaved as if he existed in the Highlands of the sixteenth century. Walter Scott knew him well; it was, in fact, Colonel MacDonell who gave Scott his famous deerhound, Maida.

Glengarry died in 1828 when attempting to escape from the wreck of a steamer on the coast near Fort William.

His funeral must have been the last of its kind in the Highlands. A howl of fury went up from his clansmen when it became known that a hearse was to be sent to take the old chief to his grave. They threatened to smash it if it should attempt to enter the glen. 'It is by the hands of his people and shoulder high', they said, 'that he should be borne to the grave. Never would we see MacOmhic-Alastair carried to Kilfinnan in a cart.'

And so it was. At sunrise on the funeral day parties of the clan came down from the hills, each section headed by the pipes. They lined up on the lawn of the castle. In front of the open door was planted a yellow standard, the clan banner, surmounted by a holly bush, the badge of Clan Donald. Four clansmen carried the coffin. Four others stood at the corners bearing flaming torches. Wax tapers had been fixed to the stags' antlers which decorated the outside of the castle. The 'ceann-tigh', the heads of the

cadet families, then took up the coffin, and, as they began to march off, Glengarry's piper, who had taken his post beside the clan banner, blew up the march 'Cille-Chriost'. It was a frightful day in the middle of January. A thunderstorm was moving over the glen. As the coffin passed through the gates a flash of lightning and a peal of thunder caused Glengarry's old blind bard, Allan Dall, to break out into a funeral dirge, waving his bonnet in the air and crying, 'Ochon, ochon, ochon,' in the storm.

When the funeral party reached the graveyard the stream was swollen to the size of a mad torrent – there was no bridge over it as there is today – and the Highlanders plunged in with the coffin. It seemed for a moment, when they reached the middle of the stream, that they would be swept away, for the coffin lurched and remained stationary as the bearers strove for a foothold. Then a loud voice was heard crying on the opposite bank. It was the chief's eldest son, Angus, giving the clan war cry. And at the sound of it the bearers pressed forward into the torrent and safely gained the bank.

The son who succeeded to the title was only ten years of age. It was soon discovered that Glengarry's attempt to carry the splendour of the sixteenth century into the bleak realities of the nineteenth had left him with debts of £80,000. There was nothing for it but to sell the estates. They were sold again in 1840 and for a third time in 1860.

And today the traditions of this great clan are to be found in Canada, where there are said to be something like 20,000 Macdonalds in Glengarry, Ontario.

I went on over the roof of the Highlands, mounting steadily, until, at the crest, the road dipped down and I ran out of the clouds and passed into the next valley – Glen Clunie.

Again I went down, down, down into one of

the loveliest glens in Scotland – Glen Shiel.

This is the 'road to the isles'. This is the way Johnson and Boswell came riding on a September day in 1773, and it was here that the Highlanders clustered round them like Red Indians as Boswell handed out bits of bread and twists of tobacco, while the large doctor lined up the children and gave them pennies. Boswell observed to Johnson that it was very much the same as being with a tribe of Indians:

'Yes, sir, but not so terrifying,' said the doctor.

So I went on to the climax: the sudden view, at the head of the glen, of Loch Duich. This is a salt-water loch that thrusts itself inland between the mountains. Its shores are gold with salt weed. I saw it with the sun on it. The sky was blue. The loch was blue. The mountains were a darker blue. Backward through the glen I saw a wild cluster of mountains with the sun shadows over their deep corries, desolate slanting uplands, deer forests, dark little valleys which the sun never touches, steep precipices streaked with thin white lines of falling water.

I was as far from civilization as it is possible to be in Great Britain. The nearest market town was Inverness, and it was over fifty miles away.

Just before the sun set I mounted the great hill above Loch Duich, the road that runs up over the summit of Mam Rattachan to the little coast town of Glenelg.

Sir John is an old friend of mine, but at times I dislike him almost as much as he, at times, dislikes me. He is tall, thin, bleakly blue of eye, and has a complexion which is a network of tiny blood vessels. His face always looks chilblained, due, I think, to the frosty nature of his prejudices. He wears shrill tweed clothes

reinforced at the shoulders with strips of leather.

He believes first of all in the divine right of kings, then in Eton and Oxford, then in the Carlton Club, then in the superiority of London under the Empire (promenade), and lastly in the Church of England. He is about sixty, but the fact that he has not given birth to an original thought since he was twenty has helped to make him appear younger. He is, therefore, happy and enviable. I like him because I think he is funny; he dislikes me because he thinks I am funny.

'Look here,' said Sir John, 'I can't for the life of me make out why you should be one of these confounded sentimentalists who are ruining the country. Come out and have a shot at a stag!'

'I won't have a shot at a stag because I used to be a marksman and I might hit him, but to prove that I'm not ruining the country I'll come out stalking with you and I'll swear not to shout, sing, wave my arms, throw stones, or in any way interfere with the assassination.'

'There you go – assassination! Can't you see, my dear fellow. . . .'

'Perfectly. You think these stags belong to you, and – what is really in your favour – you like venison, therefore you shoot stags; and I understand. I detest venison, and I like the look of stags when alive, so that for me to shoot a stag would be both untidy and criminal.'

Sir John then made that sound which writers interpret as 'Tcha!'

If fox hunting holds all the thrills of cavalry warfare, deerstalking is the infantry equivalent.

It was while we were at breakfast that a scout arrived to say that the enemy had been sighted 'on the hill'. It is usual in the Highlands to employ this vague phrase 'on the hill' to indicate square miles of mountains. (A stranger unaware of the map might think that there was

only one hill north of the Caledonian Canal!)

Breakfast, therefore, broke up in some disorder and in a few minutes the room looked like a G.H.Q. surprised by a sudden enemy offensive.

The troops had paraded near the stables. We told off the advance guard – two earnest young ghillies armed with telescopes. Sir John and I then fell in to lead the main body, composed of an odd stalker or two carrying guns and leading two shaggy Highland ponies saddled ready for the dead bodies.

So we plodded on through a wood beside a stream, over a moor and up to 'the hill'. We reached an undulating heathery space and we saw before us brown hill after brown hill, a fretted skyline of peaks, and a valley with a foaming torrent dashing through it over rocks.

We flung ourselves in the heather, opened telescopes and, lying on our backs, examined the face of a hill which was perhaps four miles off.

'Bad day,' said Sir John, 'the wind's all wrong.'
'They may get away?'
'They may! I suppose you'd enjoy that?'
'I shall smile!'
'Well, we'll see if we can't do some shooting.'
'You bloodthirsty old brute!'

Sir John turned to me a face purpled with passion, for this is the one remark you must never make to a deer-stalker. No deer-stalker regards himself as bloodthirsty so long as he rations himself to one death a day.

I saw a number of brown creatures grazing on the distant hill. They looked to me like ponies until I saw their hind-quarters. There were about thirty hinds. Some distance from them in lordly isolation was the stag, a fine fellow with an arched neck and a magnificent head.

It is now the time of year, explained one of the ghillies, when the stags roam the hills and round up the hinds. They wander about like sultans with their harems. Sometimes they meet another male, who at once challenges them. They fight. If the newcomer wins, the old sultan gallops off and leaves the victor in possession of the hinds, but sometimes their antlers become locked, and when the winter snows have melted you find on the hills the skeletons of two stags.

'What happens to the hinds when both stags are killed?'
'They just go off and get rounded up by other stags.'

While I watched the distant hill I saw our stag rise up and exert his authority. A few hinds had strayed from the herd. He pranced up, lowered his head, and said very plainly: 'Now come along, you girls must stick together,' and having brought them back he retired to his place.

'He'll do. A big chap,' said Sir John.

We then set out, leaving the ponies and the ghillies behind.

There followed two hours of enjoyable but exhausting physical hardship. If you think deer-stalking is just spotting a stag and walking cautiously for a mile or two, and then shooting him, try it. In the first place, the deer-stalker has, like the fox hunter, to be able to anticipate the actions of his quarry. He must know with tolerable certainty what the stag will do in about three hundred unforeseen circumstances. Every set of antlers is the wireless aerial which communicates to a stag in some mysterious way the latest news bulletins from the surrounding hills.

It is not necessary for the deer-stalker to be seen to be believed. The stag is an acute bundle of nerves and instincts. He smells trouble more than a mile off. The clumsy stalker has no chance. Although the wind may be blowing from him, a small gust blown back to the stag from a ledge of rock and up he springs and off he goes . . .

I felt the excitement of this stalk. There were moments when it was necessary to lie in brown streams of peaty water; there were moments when it was necessary to remain prone in the heather with one's face pressed affectionately against the hob-nailed boots of the stalker in front; there were moments when one hardly dared to breathe in case a loose stone became dislodged in a gully and, bounding down, started an avalanche which would ruin Sir John's day.

Then, weary, wet, starving, covered in mud and bleeding in places from scratches, we came after two hours' crawling, peeping, whispering, and lying about in streams, to the crest of a hill which would give us a shot at the stag. It was a steep climb through a miniature valley; just a cleft in the hill which had become filled with stunted trees and brushwood.

Sir John was interesting. His blue eyes gleamed frostily. He had in some way retained his dignity while he lay in river-beds. In an incredibly wild flight of the imagination he reminded me of some high staff-officer engaged in a desperate enterprise in no-man's-land. Not a word was said. He and the stalkers understood one another perfectly by nods and looks and liftings of the eyebrows.

The moment came when he took his loaded rifle. It was an exciting moment. I must admit that he had earned his stag. I nearly wrote on an envelope, 'Over the top and the best of luck,' but his expression forbade any such flippancy. It was deathly quiet. The wind remained on our side. Sir John began to crawl onward and upward. We lay below watching him. Every movement was important.

He was but a short distance from the crest of the hill when it happened! We saw with astonishment that something had come over the crest and was looking down at him. It was a sheep! For one awful instant the sheep and Sir John gazed into each other's eyes. Both seemed to say:

'You idiot, what are you doing there?'

Then the sheep's head disappeared, and Sir John topped the hill. He turned and waved to us. We scrambled up to him. The hillside was bare!

Not a hind! Not a stag! And no need to ask the reason why! That sheep, starting back suddenly, had given the alarm! The stag had bounded up crying:

'Come on, girls, here's Sir John!'

In one second they had streamed round the mountain-side. I admired Sir John; he had made no mistakes. I admired the stag; neither had he; and he had won.

'Well, well,' said Sir John as a stalker produced sandwiches, 'you see how it is.'

'You're a sportsman,' I said. 'I expected you to have a fit or shoot the sheep.'

'Don't be an ass,' he said. 'It's the stalking that matters. He got away. He deserved to get away. Better luck next time.'

Kipper factory, Mallaig　　　　Opposite *The Harbour, Mallaig*

The road from Kinlochaylort to Arisaig runs sometimes beside the water, then it mounts and twists among the hills; but every yard of it is beautiful with the almost supernatural beauty of the west. I can compare it only to the west coast of Ireland, where the hills have as many moods as a petulant girl.

From high places on the way to Arisaig you look out towards the strange little islands which dot the sea; the hills of Eigg rise up sharply like a wall; southward you see the abrupt ridges of the mountains in Mull; and below you is the salt water of Loch Ailort.

One of the most beautiful sights in the Western Highlands is the bright saffron weed which fringes the salt-water lochs. In the old days men made a dye from it and there are three distinct kinds of weed, each of them, I imagine, rich in iodine. This is the same weed which girls in the west of Ireland carry in great dripping creels to the potato patches.

But how impossible to find words to paint the silence, the loneliness!

I went on all through that afternoon, and when I came to a hill above Toigal I saw lying below me the mouth of the Morar River and a large bay of silver sand. I sat fascinated by the Falls of Morar, which, I think, are the finest falls I have seen in Scotland. The river was in spate. It came, moving slowly and heavily like a sheet of glass, down from the divine loch at the back; and then it just flung itself into the air and fell snow white in long wind-blown streamers.

It was getting dark as I came into that outpost of the world – Mallaig. Here is a harbour, and in the harbour a queer, stormy-looking fleet of small ships with high fo'c'sles. They smell of all the more sea-sick foods: pea soup, mutton, bacon. These are the ships that almost convince the Outer Isles that there is somewhere a place called Britain. They go out to Portree in Skye,

Loch Shiel

Next page *Borrodale, near Arisaig*

they go nosing heavily over to Harris where the tweed comes from, and to Stornoway, in Lewis, were the late Lord Leverhulme tried to modernise the Gael.

I lean over the deck of the Stornoway boat with a greater feeling of adventure than I have felt when bound for the ends of the earth. I am going to the Isle of Skye. I look out to the misty headlands, grey in a drizzle, and down into the bottle-green depths where small fish swim; and all round me is the exciting bustle of departure.

I feel, as I approach Skye, that I am on the way to wreck a dream. It may be almost as disappointing to see Skye as to meet in later life the girl you wanted to marry when you were eighteen! But something in the blue mountains reassures me as the clouds lift–queer, grotesque mountains, dark and heroic.

The boat steams in between the mainland and the island of Scalpay, and to the West loom giant peaks with a hint of darker, higher, and even wilder peaks behind them; and as the dusk falls infrequent lights gem the shore – the lights of little homes far from anywhere. There is no sound but the thrust of the steamer through the quiet seas; and a strange feeling comes out to me from the land, from the gaunt, black shadows that lie piled against the clouds, persuading me that I have left the world behind me.

I am glad that there is no one to talk to me. It is not often that a man feels himself hanging between this world and the next, between past and future, in some strange, timeless interlude. I am anxious not to exaggerate this feeling, because I cannot hope that anyone who has not felt the shadow of Skye for the first time will understand it. It would not have surprised me to see a galley put out from the dark shores and to come face to face with Ulysses or Jason . . .

We turn at last into the peace of a quiet harbour, where lights shine high up among trees. It seems to me that all the population of Portree has come down to greet the link with another world. I smell the glorious sweet reek of peat.

'Your first visit?' asks a quiet voice at my side. It is the captain, and he is about to light a pipe.

'Yes.'

'Weel – ye'll come back!' he says, and flings his match into the still harbour.

Where an ice-white salmon stream flows through a gorge to join Loch Sligachan is utter desolation, and an hotel, called an inn, which might have been blown over from Devon. Here are salmon-fishers, deer-slayers, artists in oil and water-colour, mountaineers, and the clipped voice of that which was once the English ruling class.

I arrived there after dark over nine miles of uninhabited mountain-side. I knew that I was in a wilderness. I could feel the nearness of great mountains, although I could see nothing in the mist. I could smell mountains in the wet wind as you can smell ships in a fog.

I dined and joined the varied crowd in the lounge. It seemed to me that these people had been drawn together by virtue of the wilderness outside, much as those in *The Decameron* were drawn together by the plague. You cannot stand on etiquette in a mountain hut, and this place, in spite of its hot baths, its aquatints, and its garage, was spiritually a mountain hut: the only place of warmth and shelter in the abomination of desolation.

I was awakened before the sun was up by the rush of a stream over stones. I drew the blind on a still, clear, lemon-coloured sky and a sight that made me gasp. Right in front of me a tremendous Vesuvius called Glamaig shot up

in the air, a colossal cone, with queer, grey-pink ravines searing his gigantic flanks. The rising sun immediately behind him covered him in a weird, reflected light, that hung over his vastness like gold dust. All round him, shouldering him, were other mountains, vague in morning mists, enormous shadows with white clouds steaming over their crests. Gentler moorlands, brown with heather, formed the reverse slope of that wild valley through which the ice-white stream tumbled beneath a stone bridge towards the silver waters of Loch Sligachan.

No words can tell the strange atmosphere of this place, which is unlike Scotland, unlike Norway, unlike Switzerland, unlike anything else on earth.

I dressed – but with no idea of the shock that awaited me outside!

The inn is built at an angle which, when you stand on the steps, cuts off the view to the right. You remain there, mesmerized by Glamaig, in whose shadow you stand. He is in the shape of Vesuvius. He looks as though he might at any moment give a terrible explosion and belch flame. You take a step towards him. You clear the boundary wall, and instantly out of the corner of your eye become aware of something tremendous to your right. You turn ... the sight of the 'Black' Coolins hits you like a blow in the face!

I gasped. I lost my breath. These expressions are generally untrue. You seldom gasp or lose your breath. It is a figure of speech. But when you come suddenly for the first time on the Coolins your mouth opens and you really do gasp.

Imagine Wagner's 'Ride of the Valkyries' frozen in stone and hung up like a colossal screen against the sky. It seems as if Nature when she hurled the Coolins up into the light of the sun said: 'I will make mountains which shall be the essence of all that can be terrible in mountains. I will pack into them all the fearful mystery of high places. I will carve them into a million queer, horrible shapes. Their scarred ravines, on which nothing shall grow, shall lead up to towering spires of rock, sharp splinters shall strike the sky along their mighty summits, and they shall be formed of rock unlike any other rock so that they will never look the same for very long, now blue, now grey, now silver, sometimes seeming to retreat or to advance, but always drenched in mystery and terrors.

It takes time for the mind to adjust itself to the Coolins. Some minds, I imagine, never become reconciled to them, but feel always that a spectre is walking at their side. I can imagine a neurotic person flying from these mountains as from the devil.

I understand, and feel, the fascination which they exert over others.

I sit in candle-light in the inn at Portree waiting for a ghost. It is a wild, gusty night. The rain beats up in sudden fury against the window. It is just such a night as that, many years ago, on which Prince Charlie said good-bye to Flora Macdonald in this room. . . .

It was nearly midnight. The wind shook at the window, and the rain fell, as rain can fall only in Skye. Into the candle-light of this room came the Prince, flying from Kingsburgh House, and no longer disguised as Flora Macdonald's Irish maid. On his way here he had gladly entered a wood to step from the flowered linen gown and the quilted petticoat which he wore so clumsily. He put on Highland dress – a tartan coat, waistcoat, filabeg, hose, a plaid, a wig, and a bonnet.

He was drenched to the skin. He called for a dram of spirits, and then changed into a dry

shirt. The innkeeper had no idea of his rank, or, if so, kept his mouth shut, as everyone did in the Highlands. He set before the visitor fish, bread, and cheese. In those awful days after Culloden Prince Charlie seemed to have a song or a laugh always on his lips. He joked with the good man, and trying to change a guinea could get only thirteen shillings for it!

Half a mile away a rowing-boat beached in the dark pointed to the island of Raasay. Men came secretly to the little room and implored the Prince to go. There was £30,000 in English gold on his head, and though the poorest man in the Highlands would not have touched a penny of it, who knew what dangerous Hanoverian might seek shelter in the Portree inn on such a fiendish night? The Prince listened to the rain and the wind. Perhaps he walked to the window, as I have just done, and saw the dark bay below, sheeted in blown mist, and the trees bent back from the land. Could he not stay the night and set out in the dawn? Impossible! They would not hear of it! All right, he would come, but – first he must smoke a pipe of tobacco!

Can you imagine how they fumed and fretted as the young man calmly lit his pipe, and how every creak on the stairs must have seemed like the step of some enemy creeping in the dark; and how often did they tiptoe to the door to listen, with their thoughts on the window and the drop beneath?

He knocked out his pipe and rose. He was ready! He turned to the brave woman who had saved his life and said good-bye. He gave her his miniature and repaid a small sum of money which he had borrowed from her. Then this wet, hunted prince smiled and said, magnificently, that in spite of all that had happened he hoped some day to welcome her to St. James's!

Is there a more operatic farewell in history? Think of him standing there in the candle-light, hunted, beaten, bedraggled, in borrowed clothes, £30,000 on his head and all England after him, holding a parcel containing four clean shirts, a cold fowl tied in a handkerchief, a bottle of brandy on one side of his belt, a bottle of whisky on the other, going out in the rain with an invitation to Court on his lips!

So Flora Macdonald watched him leave the candle-light for the dark of the stairhead, heard the cautious steps and the shutting of the inn door and the tramp of feet beneath the window.

I wait for the ghost. I wait for the door to be flung open; but all I see is a vision of my own making: Flora Macdonald standing there, holding the miniature, still warm from his hands.

Loch Scavaig and the Coolins, Skye

5
Ben Nevis
Glencoe

It was one of those mornings that arrive suddenly in the Highlands after a week of drizzle: a day of atonement, a day that wipes out memories of rain as freedom from it can obliterate even the memory of neuralgia. The rowan berries were red as blood in Glen Spean. The river, winding its way over moss-grown stones and foaming over rocks, lay smooth in shallow places like melted green glass. After Roy Bridge I saw the sun falling upon wide moorlands where the heather was dying and the fern was russet brown. I had decided to walk across the Corrieyarrick.

Sir John Cope's failure to command the Corrieyarrick in 1745 and his futile recruiting march to Inverness, which opened the south to Charlie's army, was a mistake so unaccountable and so farcical that no wonder it was whispered in England that Johnny Cope was a Jacobite. Poor honest, dull John Cope! It is a fact, however, that this Hanoverian general's mistake did more to give the Jacobite Rebellion a sporting chance than all the English Jacobites put together.

A narrow track ended at Garva Bridge, where a shallow hill torrent came streaming down over boulders, and ahead lay a bleak stretch of bogland and heather. The old road was at once visible. It is about six feet wide and the great blocks of stone, which the English troops put down two hundred years ago, are lying in peat water with grass growing between them. My back ached to think of the labour of making the road over the Corrieyarrick, through one of the most desolate hill passes in Scotland. The road mounts and twists, loses itself, finds itself, and

Ben Nevis: the Tower Ridge

Next page *Ben Nevis and the Caledonian Canal*

runs like an Alpine road round the very edge of a precipice; then it strikes off over the heather and goes striding up towards the sky over the great shoulder of Garbh Beinn.

A dead road always fills me with melancholy. If, as someone has said, civilization is transportation, then a dead road is symbolic of the end of all things. One looks at it and wonders what in all this world is safe from the nettle and the thistle. Yet the dead road over the Corrieyarrick is not pitiful in quite the same way that the Appian Way is pitiful, or as the Peddars' Way in Norfolk is pitiful, because it was never more than a military highway and the only ghosts likely to be met with on it would be redcoats plodding wearily to the tap of a drum.

This dead road makes one realize two things: the terrible hardship of a military campaign in the Highlands and the tremendous work accomplished by Field-Marshal George Wade when he built those now mostly grass-grown tracks which are indicated by the words 'Gen. Wade's Road' on the Ordnance Survey maps of Scotland. Every Highlander should know something of George Wade, because it was over his roads that the Macs have advanced from their hereditary fastnesses to premierships, banks, limited liability companies, engineering works, newspaper offices, and so on, all over the world.

The failure of the road in 1745 is clear from a contemporary description: 'It is plain that a very small Force, who were Masters of this Hill, were capable of stopping or even defeating a considerable Army that should attempt to dislodge them. For, each Traverse, in ascending, is commanded by that above it; so that even an unarmed Rabble, who were posted on the higher ground, might without exposing themselves, extremely harass the Troops on their March. Whence the attempting to force seventeen traverses, every one of them capable of being so defended, was an Undertaking which

it would have been Madness to have engaged in, with a Number inferior to the Highlanders from their Knowledge of the Country, their natural Agility, and their Attachment to Ambushes and Skirmishes, would, in this Situation, have indulged their Genius, and would, doubtless, have proved most formidable Opponents. Besides, could it be supposed that by the Bravery of the Troops, or an uncommon Share of good Fortune, all these Passes had been cleared and the Army had arrived on the top of the Corriarrick, yet, the Descent would have been still more hazardous, and, if the aforementioned Bridge was broken down, became absolutely impossible; for then neither a Carriage, nor a Baggage Horse could have crossed the Hollow.'

Fort William nestles, or crouches, with an air of pretending to be the end of the world at the foot of Ben Nevis, the highest and most famous mountain in the British Isles. It is 4,406 feet in height, or 846 feet higher than Snowdon. Every healthy man who visits Fort William climbs Ben Nevis. No one suggests that he should do so. It is just one of Scotland's unwritten laws of decent conduct. When he has done this the climber finds that the atmosphere of Fort William warms towards him. He went up friendless; he returns to smiles and companionship. He has proved himself.

Men who previously scowled uncertainly at him now regard his torn and battered feet with approval and say, 'You've been up "the Ben"!' He finds that he has earned the confidences of other men who have climbed Ben Nevis. He learns with respectful disappointment that he has put up no new record; that hefty local Scotsmen have gone up and come down in a quarter of the time; but no matter! He went up

a novice; he returns initiated as one of that noble company who know the summit of Britain's greatest mountain.

Before I set off I walked round Fort William in the hope of seeing Ben Nevis; but nothing is more difficult. I have never found it so hard to see a mountain. The Ben has a base which is said to be twenty-four miles in circumference, so that firmly seated on this rocky throne he manages to hide his crown in mist or beyond the shoulders of lesser monarchs.

As I walked singing up the glen with a heart as foolishly light as my shoes, a woman at the white farm of Achintree, holding a baby in a tartan kilt, smiled and said, 'It's a graund day for "the Ben",' and as she said it she looked up into the sky in the direction of the invisible summit. 'A graund day for "the Ben"'! They all talk about Ben Nevis as if he were an aged and irascible old gentleman whose polite reception of the stranger is by no means guaranteed!

And this, I was to learn, is the best way to regard him!

The sun shines. It is warm. The distant trees are turning goldy-brown, and as I mount the winding path the sound of the burn that curves and twists through Glen Nevis grows fainter and finally ceases.

I am alone in the sunlight with great hills shouldering the sky above me, brown with dead bracken, grey with the beautiful silvery heather stems, and soggy with peat bogs. Birds fly up from the heather; sheep look up from their grazing with no expression, and thrusting their soft bodies into the heather continue to crop the grass. Little brown peaty streams rumble from above and fall cascading between boulders down the hill-side.

There comes in the climbing of all mountains a time when a man turns to face the loneliness of great hills and that solitude which never has given and never will give food or shelter to man. The hills shoulder one another as if to cut off sight of the habitable earth; the clouds loom nearer; the yellow clouds which from earth are puffy cotton-wool things are now seen to have texture, to be wind-blown in wild spirals; the darker clouds are misty and frayed at the edges with impending rain and the grass grows thinner, the rock more frequent, and the wind is cold.

So yard by flinty yard I mount slowly and painfully into a grim valley of rocks through which falls a stream. I am now on a level with the lesser mountains; I can even see above their heads beyond to hills and more hills and a hint of water.

I come to a little tarn hidden in the mountains, lying there all silent like a patch of fallen blue sky, and near it is the half-way hut.

The path now grows steeper, its zigzags more frequent, its surface rougher; and I go on full of a magnificent exhilaration, the cold air like wine. When I turn to look back I find some new marvel: a sudden gleam of the Atlantic over a mountain's head; dim, blue, far-off peaks that may be the Hebrides. Then, suddenly, I am in a valley of death. Nothing grows. The bare rock thrusts its sharp edges from the mountain-side. The clouds are near. There is even one far below

Ben Nevis, across Loch Linnhe

me, a thin grey thing, gently steaming over the face of the mountain, a stray, lost wisp of a cloud.

I am so far above the world of man that even the sunlight does not cheer this solitude. The spirit of great mountains is a wild, implacable spirit. Even the jolly golden clouds that sail so near can come before the sun and in an instant be things of horrible mystery, ominous things hiding something that might obliterate a man on a mountain-side as a bird picks a fly from a wall.

Man is nowhere so alone with all the fears in his blood as on the side of a mountain.

I tramp on with bursting lungs, beating heart, and lacerated feet, my mind fixed on the summit that surely cannot be far off!

Suddenly the sunlight dies. I enter a mist: a thin, clinging mist, a cold, foggy mist. I am warm with my climb. I do not notice how cold it is. Out of it emerge two shapes. Two men come towards me muffled to the eyes. They wear gloves and their teeth are chattering, their noses are red, their ears stand out like slices of raw beef. They try to smile but the smile freezes on their iced cheeks:

'Another half mile!' they say to me. 'Is it still fine down below?'

'Yes, brilliant sun!'

They swing their arms like cabmen on a frosty morning, and, taking off their gloves, blow into their cold fingers.

'Don't lean on the wooden platform over the ravine. It's not safe! Good-bye!'

And they depart, fading in the mist. As I go on the mist thickens. There are irregular patches of snow two or three inches deep. I have come into the depth of winter. An icy wind howls round me, whipping the chill mist into my face. All the heat of my climb is taken out of me. I stoop in the wind and take out a coat from my knapsack and cover myself; but I am now so cold that I cannot feel my ears; and my eyes ache.

The mist turns to sleet, and the sleet to soft, whirling snow that dances giddily round me on every side. The path becomes level. Through the snow I see the ruin of a stone house. I go in for shelter. It is a horrible ruin, like a ship-wreck. It looks as if all the fiends of the air have torn it stone from stone. I hear the most horrible sound on earth – the sough of wind coming up over the crest of Ben Nevis. It is not loud. I have to listen for it, and having heard it I go on listen-ing with chilled blood: it is a dreadful sound; an evil, damnable sound. I am drawn towards it through the snow. I come to the jagged edge of the mountain. The snow is whirled up over the edge of it. It is as if the snow were rising and not falling; and all the time the wind comes moan-ing out of space over the edge of Ben Nevis.

The precipice is 1,500 feet deep. I take a stone and fling it. Seven sickening seconds and then, far off, an echo of the fall and another and another.

I stand chilled to the very marrow, watching the weird snowfall veer and shift in the wind, blowing aside to reveal dim, craggy shapes, rocks like spectres or crouching men or queer, misshapen beasts. And the dreadful ghost of a wind moaning over the precipice with an evil invitation at the back of it, moaning up out of space, through distant spiky gullies where the sun is shining, moaning with a suggestion of inhuman mirth, causes me to face the ravine as if something might come out of it which would have to be fought.

I could stay there longer if the wind would not bite into my bones and numb my fingers. I go on out of the snow and into the sleet and the mist. And on my way down a great hole is suddenly blown in the cloud, and I see, it seems at my feet, an amazing, brilliant panorama of mountains with the sun on them, of blue lochs, a steamer no bigger than a fly moving up Loch Ness beneath the arch of a rainbow. Then the hole fills with mist and I go on for an hour, stumbling, scrambling until the mist frays and stops, and the sun shines . . .

All round me are the Highlands, magnificent among the clouds, the evening blueness spread-ing over them; peak calling to peak, the Atlantic like a thin streak of silver, the bare rock beneath my feet fading to brown bogland and heather.

I sit down and hold out my frozen hands in the sun, and, suddenly catching sight of my shoes, which have in their time known Piccadilly and Bond Street, I roar with laughter!

Fort William was transformed. Its streets were full of kilted men. Grants walked with Frazers, MacLeans with MacKinnons, Mac-kenzies with Mackintoshs; in fact, a casual scrutiny seemed to suggest that every clan feud had been healed except, of course, that of MacDonald and Campbell.

The hotel lounge, so recently an abode of peace, was full of Highlanders. The bar was also full. Everyone was talking about the Mod, about choirs, about recitations. Men came in swinging their tartan kilts. Everybody knew everybody else. It was a cheerful gathering of the clans.

The kilt dignifies every occasion. Even a fat man groping in a sporran to find a shilling to pay for his tea cannot appear ridiculous. While the Welsh Eisteddfod brings to mind hundreds of men in their best blue serge suits, the Gaelic Mod will always remind me of clan tartan.

A number of the more earnest Gaels had, I learnt, arrived from London only that morning. They were mostly middle-aged men in beauti-fully cut Highland garments, huge Cairngorms shining in the hafts of the skean dhus and their black brogues laced with leather thongs.

Glencoe

Next page *Loch Leven*

founded in 1891 to preserve and develop the speech, music, folk-art and industry of the Scottish Gael. In other words, the Mod is to the Highlands exactly what the Eisteddfod is to Wales: an annual feast of song at which people who speak two languages – English and their mother tongue – assemble to warm their hands at the fire of a common racial culture.

Along the road from Ballachulish where the river Coe pours into Loch Leven is a comfortable little village which boasts the most grotesque signpost in the British Isles:

THE VILLAGE OF GLENCOE
SCENE OF THE FAMOUS MASSACRE
TEAS AND REFRESHMENTS
TOBACCO AND CIGARETTES

'Are they playing like children at a fancy dress party,' I wondered, 'or is this real? No doubt these men were to be found in London yesterday wearing trousers and behaving like normal Londoners, with nothing about them save perhaps a Gaelic softness in the speech to distinguish them from their fellows. Now look at them swaggering in their clan tartans.'

When I entered the bar a ring of heated Highland faces presented itself. Voices were loud in argument and in story. All the arguments were abstract and all the stories about people who were dead! This Mod, I said to myself, is more interesting than the Eisteddfod of the Welsh because it is a social reunion as well as an artistic one. In Wales they do not waste time filling the bars with laughter and with argument; it would ruin their wind. But here at the Mod, so it seemed to me, the meeting of the clans was just as important as the music which was the official reason for the meeting.

What is the Mod, and how did it begin?

The word means 'gathering'. It is the annual assembly of An Comunn Gaidhealach, a society

This statement relieves the feeling of gloom with which a traveller approaches the scene of the clan massacre. The only writer who found Glencoe cheerful was Andrew Lang. Macaulay's description is well known, so is that by Dorothy Wordsworth; perhaps the best, however, is the not so familiar letter by Dickens in Forster's *Life*.

'All the way,' wrote Dickens, 'the road had been among moors and mountains with huge masses of rock which fell down God knows where, sprinkling the ground in every direction, and giving it the aspect of the burial place of a race of giants. Now and then we passed a hut or two, with neither window nor chimney, and the smoke of the peat fire rolling out at the door.

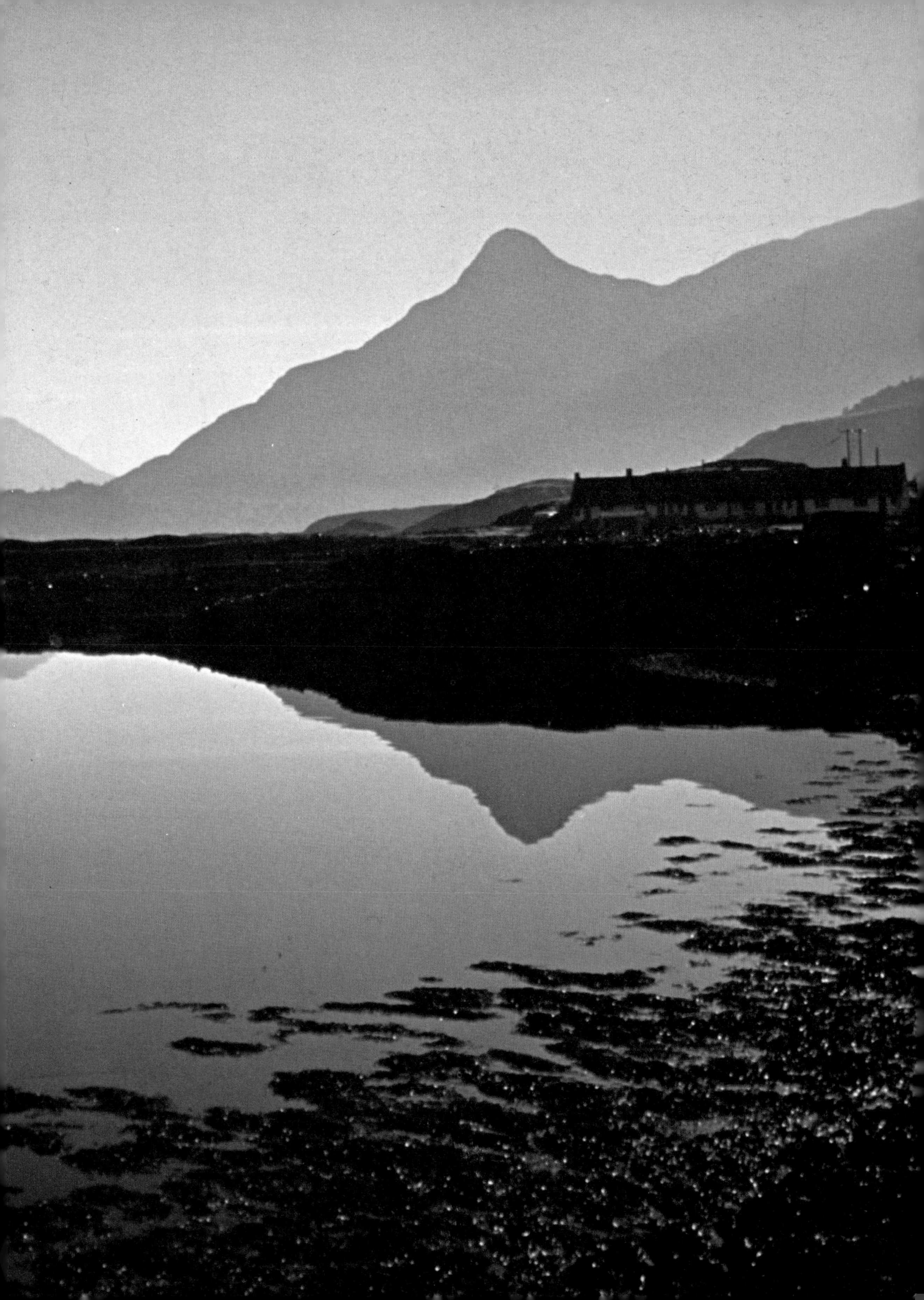

Loch Leven and the Pap of Glencoe

Next page *Glencoe, towards the Three Sisters*

But there were not six of these dwellings in a dozen miles; and anything so bleak and wild and mighty in its loneliness, as the whole country, it is impossible to conceive. Glencoe itself is perfectly *terrible*. The pass is an awful place. It is shut in on each side by enormous rocks from which great torrents come rushing down in all directions. In amongst these rocks on one side of the pass (the left as we came) there are scores of glens, high up, which form such haunts as you might imagine yourself wandering in, in the very height and madness of a fever. They will live in my dreams for years – I was going to say as long as I live, and I seriously think so. The very recollection of them makes me shudder. . . .'

I went on into this mountain pass ready, even anxious, to shudder at it. But, alas, the sun was shining! Glencoe in this mood – the mood that Lang must have known – is not frightful: it is awesome, it is stark, it is, like all the wild mountains of Scotland, a lesson in humility. Man has never existed for it; it is, at least in sunlight, not unfriendly so much as utterly oblivious of humanity.

The volcanic heights are gashed by sharp gullies, broadening as they descend, in which water has in the course of centuries found its way to the valley. In some of these gashes trees try to hide from the wind like men sheltering. Mostly they are great slashes in the rock, as if giants had sharpened their swords on the hills . . .

The sun is covered by a cloud. The light dies in Glencoe as suddenly as a light is switched off in a room. The pass has changed colour. It is grey and hopeless. Now you see why Macaulay called it the 'Valley of the Shadow'. As you look up at the mountains, at the queer gullies and the dark glens they seem a fit abode for naked devils. It was surely in such a place as Glencoe that the Gadarene swine met their end.

6
Mull
Arran
Loch Lomond
Glasgow

Oban, more than any town on the west coast of Scotland, is a place of happy memories.

It is from Oban that thousands of people set out to visit the enchanted Western Isles which lie out in the Atlantic and do not seem to belong to this world. It is to Oban that the little steamers bring back travellers from the west.

I took the road north-east from Oban and came to the ruins of a great castle which stands on a promontory where Lock Linnhe enters Loch Etive. This was the famous stronghold of Dunstaffnage. It is from this old ruin that the Captain of Dunstaffnage takes his ancient title.

It has been a magnificent castle: now it is merely a shell with nine-foot-thick walls from which is one of the finest views on the west coast.

Stand, as I did, in the afternoon of one of those summer days that swing in from the Atlantic in October, and you will never forget the crumbling ramparts of Dunstaffnage. You look eastward up Loch Etive towards the twin peaks of Ben Cruachan; westward over the narrow sea are the blue mountains of Mull and Morven; to the north is Loch Nell with its fringe of saffron weed.

The greatest memory of Dunstaffnage is that of the Coronation Stone, which is today in Westminster Abbey beneath that famous chair on which so many schoolboys have carved their names. This stone was the ancient Coronation stone of the Irish kings. It was said to have been Jacob's pillow on the plains of Luz.

When the Scots came over from Ireland to settle in Caledonia they brought this stone

Highland cattle on the banks of Loch Etive

Next page *Buachaille Etive Mor*

125

with them, first to Iona and then to Dunstaffnage, which became the capital of the Dalriadic kingdom. Afterwards, when Scone became the capital, the Stone of Destiny went there, and remained from 850 until the year 1297, when Edward I removed it to Westminster Abbey.

There is another memory in this castle. In 1746 a boat came over from the Western Isles bringing Flora Macdonald as a state prisoner to Dunstaffnage. She was on her way to London to be tried for helping Prince Charles Edward to escape after Culloden.

I have spent two days wandering about the Isle of Mull, and during that time I have met on the roads perhaps ten people. The great hills rise up over the island, clothed with green almost to their summits, and above them, and never for long invisible, is Ben More, the presiding giant of Mull. He is an extinct volcano. From his lofty crater poured out the molten masses that have cooled into the weird and massive columns in the south of Mull.

The roads dip down in silence through dark valleys, they rise up to wild moorlands where the heather is dying, they wind round lovely sheets of water cupped in a hollow of the hills; and all this land is as it left the hand of God.

You are never far from salt water. You climb a hill, or you turn a bend in the road, and there before you is the Sound of Mull with the mountains of Morven rising to the north, and over the calm waters, distant and small as a floating willow leaf, is the steamer that goes to Scotland once a day.

Mull is a solemn, beautiful place; an island to which a man should go for what the Catholics call examination of conscience. There is nothing pagan about it as there is about Skye. If something should appear from behind the great

boulders that lie in the valleys and on the hills of Skye, it would be a Norse god, armed and bloodthirsty; but if Mull is haunted I feel that a man might meet an Irish saint, his sandals brushing through the dying heather.

Iona has made the Sign of the Cross over Mull.

You come across the ruins of houses, because Mull is full of deserted clachans. There may be only a few stones piled together, or a space of beaten earth on which the thorns grow, to tell you that fifty or a hundred years ago a little Highland village stood there.

Mull suffered bitterly during that disgraceful chapter in Scottish history, the evictions, when families were turned from their homes and the thatch burnt over them.

The result is that Mull is the deserted home of a great family of MacLeans (and MacLaines) who all over the world, and particularly in Canada and New Zealand, retain some memory of this island although they may never have set foot in it.

This clan is one of the most ancient and interesting in the Highlands, and in loyalty and pride is second to no other clan. The whole of Mull is strewn with memories of its warlike deeds; in fact there can be hardly a square mile of Mull which tradition does not claim as the scene of some reckless act of gallantry or cunning.

Iona and Lindisfarne and Tintagel are to me three of the most splendid names in Great Britain. Iona is the sweetest. It has the west wind in it, not the wind that runs through trees, but the wind that goes over rocks beside the sea. There is also, I think, the sound of bells in it, not church bells but the little bronze bells like sheep bells which St. Patrick and the Irish saints rang in the morning of faith.

Cottages at Treshnish, Mull

A tomb on Iona

Next page *Kilchurn Castle, Loch Awe*

In the history of Christianity there is no more lovely chapter than the coming of the Word from Ireland to Scotland and from Scotland to the north of England. There was no sound in these islands but the breaking of boughs as the Saxon war bands forced their way through the overgrown Roman cities, and no sound on the sea coasts but the cries of the Ancient Britons as they beached their coracles on the saffron weed of western lochs.

And in this time the Irish monks set out to clothe the land with Christ. They tramped the wild roads of Europe. They founded churches in Cologne, in Namur, in Liège, in Strasbourg, in Switzerland; and they crossed the Alps and saw Rome. There are believed to be sixty kings buried on Iona: forty-eight are said to be Scottish, eight are Norwegian, and four are Irish. They were buried in three great chapels, which have now vanished. The long lines of their tombstones are ranged in rows. They are green with age and defaced by the winds of centuries. Macbeth lies there and so does his royal victim, Duncan.

As one looks at these tombs it is not difficult to imagine the coming of the dead kings to the sacred isle.

They were landed at a little bay a few hundred yards from the royal burial-ground. Their funeral boats would come slowly over the Sound of Iona to the plucking of harp strings. The Irish monks, their heads shaven from ear to ear across the crown, would meet them on the white sands. There would be chanting and incense, and the bodies would be carried over that paved road, now partly hidden, but still known as 'the Street of the Dead'.

It is to St. Columba, or Columcille, that the mind returns always in Iona. He left Ireland, so it is said, either willingly or as an exile for his share in the Battle of Culdremne in 561, or, as one story goes, because he quarrelled over a copy of a sacred book; and he went in search of a place from which he could no longer see his native land. There is a legend that he landed on one of the outer isles, or on the Mull of Kintyre, but when he mounted a hill he could still see Ireland, so the long boat again put out to sea. It came to rest in Iona.

He was big, dark, and bearded, of immense physique, tireless and commanding, with a voice that could be heard reciting the psalms over phenomenal distances. There are stories that prove that he had a temper and also a sense of humour. He was probably a typical Irishman.

My favourite legend is the grimly amusing story of the foundation of St. Oran's chapel. Columba, it is said, received a heavenly message that a human victim must be buried alive in the foundations. As soon as this was known a saintly monk, Oran, offered himself, or, as other versions of the story have it, was chosen by lot. He was buried alive.

Three days afterwards Columba, who was deeply attached to Oran, dug open his grave in order to take a last look at his friend. He found Oran quite fit and well. Oran said:

'There is no wonder in death, and hell is not as it is reported.'

This unorthodoxy so horrified Columba that he hastily took a spade and reburied his friend with the words:

'Earth, earth, fill the mouth of Oran that he may gossip no more!'

St. Columba died in 597, shortly after St. Augustine had reluctantly landed in Kent with orders to convert the Anglo-Saxons. His body was buried in Iona, and a century after translated to Ireland. His remains then disappeared. Some say that they were returned to Iona and buried secretly, but it is more probable that they were scattered, a bone here and there, over Celtic Christendom.

Inverary lies on the edge of Loch Fyne like a relic of the feudal age. It is the seat – one almost writes royal seat – of the Campbells of Argyll and above the thick trees of the lochside rise the four flanking turrets of the Castle from which, when the Duke is at home, flies the standard of Argyll.

The little town lies on a pretty curve of land that thrusts itself into the waters of the loch. Neat whitewashed buildings expose demure faces to the loch and to the smooth, green hills that lie against each other, closing in the view on all sides. There is one main street, a wide, hilly street lined with modest houses and shops, including one or two full of those tartan odds and ends which the visitors from pleasure steamers presumably buy in order to prove that they have been far from home. But there is over Inveraray a respectful hush as if someone had just coughed deferentially. There is much the same hush over Balmoral and, to a lesser degree, over Sandringham.

I wandered about Inveraray, admiring the calm loch, the gentle hills, the placid main street, exploring the old court house and the gaol and the building, once a law court and now estate offices, in which a Campbell jury condemned Stewart of Appin to death. Then I went for a walk through a wood and up a hill. In all Scotland there are no finer trees than those around Inveraray. Oaks as immense as those in Windsor Great Park, beech and ash as splendid as any in the New Forest, and firs and limes by the thousand, stood in close belts of dark woodland; and it was with delight that I caught sight of the loch shining through the trees and, far below, the little French-looking town white on the loch's edge.

Down the hill again to the town and the little empty main street. It looked as if waiting for the Duke to march past behind his pipers, with banners flying and claymores white in the sun.

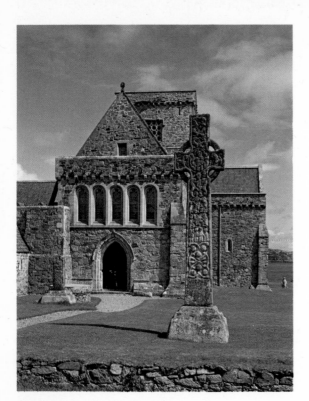

Iona Abbey

Opposite *Tobermory, Mull*

I went into the post office to send some telegrams. While I was waiting for change I wandered to the door. The only figure in the high street was a man on a bicycle who came free-wheeling down the hill at considerable speed. He wore a kilt. It was the first time I had ever seen a kilted cyclist.

'Who is that?' I asked the girl in the post office.

'Oh,' she said, 'that's his Grace.'

The Isle of Arran is the top of a submerged mountain range that lies beneath the Firth of Clyde, and the highest peak is a big brute called Goatfell. This mountain broods over the island like a threat or, perhaps, a challenge.

A hundred years ago the Gaelic was spoken in Arran, the runrig system was in operation, there were no fences or walls, panniers slung over the backs of ponies and sledges were the usual methods of haulage, the people used to wear skin moccasins like those still worn by the islanders of Aran off the west coast of Galway, and on many a windless day men could see a thin spire of smoke rising from the hills, marking an illicit still.

Superficially, I suppose, Arran has changed. The old 'black houses' have gone and there are ugly white houses. There are good roads. There are a few cars. There are post offices, and throughout the season various west-coast steamers, which carry on the work of Highland communication begun by General Wade, come slipping into Lamlash Bay from the Outer Isles or, performing a less ambitious voyage, deposit on the shores of Arran the annual quota of discerning strangers.

Essentially, however, Arran remains unchanged. Modern transport has linked her to the mainland, but spiritually she belongs to the Western Isles. In the winter time, when the storms come howling over Kilbrannan Sound from the Atlantic Ocean, it would not surprise me to hear that the Gaelic awakens over the firesides of Arran.

One of the chief glories of the island is Glen Sannox. Here are three miles of the wildest Highland scenery that can be imagined. The hills rise up on each side of the glen, bare, steep and terrible. At first you compare this glen with Glencoe, but your second thought will be more accurate: Glen Sligachan in Skye. It has the same desolate grandeur, the same eerie quality, the same air of the world's end. I am afraid I may not have expressed this very clearly. In Glencoe one has the knowledge, grand and terrific as it is, that the awesomeness is not permanent. One knows, just as the traveller in a dark tunnel is aware that the end of the tunnel is not far off, that Glencoe will end in the softness of Ballachulish. But in Glen Sligachan it is different. There is something almost hypnotic in this glen. One goes through it conscious of the terrifying Coolins and with the feeling that the end of it should be some queer unearthly blue land washed by a light not of sun or moon and inhabited by strange fabulous birds and beasts. Little Glen Sannox in Arran is the only other glen I know which possesses this same eerie quality.

I once came down through Crianlarich and Balquhidder to the clean town of Callander, which is the gate to the Trossachs.

What a country is Scotland for presiding memories. The Border is Scott, Ayr is Burns, Edinburgh is Mary, the Highlands are Prince Charlie, and the Trossachs and Loch Lomond are Rob Roy.

Scotland is a baffling country to describe. You think that you have summed her up, that you have assessed her values and reached a decision about her when without warning she suddenly flings a surprise at you. The Trossachs are not fair. A man spends months touring a country, penetrating its remote mountains, enduring heat, cold, fatigue, high teas, Sabbaths, kirks, and at the end comes suddenly on the whole thing in concentrated form, boiled down to the very essence and spread out over a small compass conveniently near to the cities of Glasgow and Edinburgh. No wonder most travellers in Scotland never get farther than the Trossachs.

How many times have I said to myself, 'That is the finest sight in Scotland.' Once again I said it on the shores of Loch Earn, as the sun was setting in a smoulder of fiery cloud, Ben Vorlich and Stuc-a-Chroin changing colour as the light goes from the sky, a water-bird winging its way to the reeds of the shore, low over the water, jet-black against the brightening silver of the loch.

In Balquhidder Churchyard is a grave they call Rob Roy's, but I should have said that the tombstone carved with a cross, a sword, and a kilted man is much older than the eighteenth century. Some one had placed a bunch of flowers on this stone. I cannot help feeling that excellent as Scott's *Rob Roy* is, and high as it stands among his novels as a literary achievement it does not do full justice to its hero. The introduction is admirable, and the Highland scenes perfect. But how sparingly Scott used the Rob

Roy legends! What annoying restraint he employed!

I re-read the novel before I entered the Mac-Gregor Country.

Rob Roy seems to sum up the Highlands just as the Trossachs sum up Scotland. How surprised Addison or Pope would have been, as Scott remarks, to know that a character who blended wild virtues with the subtle restraint and the unrestrained licence of an American Indian existed with them in the polished age of Queen Anne and George I! Imagine Robin Hood or Hereward the Wake in the England of that time! Rob Roy was the Robin Hood of Scotland, and he died as recently as 1734! He left the world just two years after James Watt entered it; it is extraordinary to think that the steam engine and Rob Roy almost coincided!

There are many fine stories of the attempts made to capture Rob Roy from time to time by the forces of the Crown and also by private individuals. There was a stout fellow who swore that with six men he would go through the Highlands and arrest the terrible Rob and bring him to jail at Stirling. The party, armed with cudgels, arrived at the public-house at Balquhidder and asked the way to Rob's house. The landlord, of course, sent word that a party of strangers was on the road so that Rob might be ready for them.

When the brave messenger arrived at the house he pretended to be a traveller who had lost his way. He was shown politely into a large room full of swords, battle-axes, hunting-horns, and trophies of the chase. When the door shut he screamed with terror to see hanging there, and intentionally placed there, the stuffed figure of a man. The enormous Rob calmly told him that it was the body of a rascally messenger who had come to his house the night before and there had been no time to bury him!

The affair ended for the messenger, as so many attempts to capture Rob Roy ended, in the river!

Surely the most extraordinary event in Rob's adventurous life was his visit to London. I cannot imagine why Scott made no use of this. The story of this visit is given in *Historical Memoirs of Rob Roy and the Clan MacGregor* by R. Macleay, in which the author writes:

'The numerous exploits of Rob Roy had rendered him so remarkable, that his name became familiar everywhere; and he was frequently the subject of conversation among the nobility at court. He was there spoken of as the acknowledged protégé of Argyll, who often endeavoured to palliate his errors; but that nobleman was frequently rallied, particularly by the king, for his partiality for MacGregor. On several occasions His Majesty had expressed a desire to see the hardy mountaineer; and Argyll, willing to gratify him, sent for Rob Roy, but concealed his being in London, lest the officers of state, aware of the king's hatred, might take measures to detain him. Argyll, however, took care that the king should see him without knowing who he was, and for this purpose made Rob Roy walk for some time in front of St. James's. His Majesty observed, and remarked that he had never seen a finer-looking man in a Highland dress, and Argyll having soon after waited on the king, his majesty told him of his having noticed a handsome Scots Highlander, when Argyll replied that it was Rob Roy MacGregor, His Majesty said he was disappointed that he did not know it sooner, and appeared not to relish the information, considering it as too serious a jest to be played upon his authority, and one which seemed to make him, among others, a dupe to our hero's impudence.'

Rob Roy in his kilt loitering at the bottom of St. James's Street is a fit companion picture to that of Prince Charlie in the Strand!

Clachan Bridge

Bottom *Brodick, Isle of Arran*

Loch Lomond.

Here is one of the world's glories. The hills lie against one another fading into the blue distance; the autumn leaves, russet, red, and gold, go down to the edge of the water, and Loch Lomond lies for twenty-four miles in exquisite beauty.

The 'bonnie, bonnie banks' are the hail and farewell of the Highlands. If you go north along the west coast it is 'Ave!' that Ben Vorlich shouts to you as he lifts his great head to the sky; if you go down from the north over the mountains it is 'Vale!' that he cries—farewell to the Highlands of Scotland! And in Loch Lomond are gathered a million beauties: soft green banks and braes; a whisper of woodland; regal mountains with the ermine of white clouds round their purple shoulders; and always, mile after mile, silver water widening to the south where islands lie at anchor like a green flotilla.

As you stand at the edge of this greatest of all British lakes watching the small waves break on the brown stones, listening to them too, marvelling that all this should be so near to Glasgow, it seems to you that Glasgow should never lose its soul. There is no excuse for it with Loch Lomond on the doorstep and Ben Lomond standing midway above the waters like a fanfare of trumpets.

A man can go out from Glasgow and climb this mountain and see Scotland; he can see his own country lying for miles in a chain of dim blue monsters. Where the eye fails him the mind can carry on, leaping in imagination from peak to peak across the Grampians, leaping from far Ben Nevis to the peaks of the Western Isles, and back across the sea to Cairn Gorm and over Scotland to those guardian ranges of the east which sometimes lie at the edge of the sea painted in the blue of heaven. What a spiritual adventure is Ben Lomond on the doorstep of Glasgow!...

Loch Lomond near Tarbet

Glasgow on a November evening ...

The fog which has tickled the throat all day relents a little and hangs thinly over the city, so that each lamp casts an inverted V of light downward on the pavement. The streets are full of light and life. Pavements are packed to the edge with men and women released from a day's work, anxious to squeeze a little laughter from the dark as they move against a hazy blur of lit windows in which lie cakes, watches, rings, motor-cars, silk gowns, and everything that is supposed to be worth buying.

I go on through the crowds. George Square— Glasgow's Trafalgar Square—which looks like the centre of the city but is not, lies in graduated greyness, rather empty, a little removed from the main surge of life, the splendid Municipal Buildings wrapped in that same aloofness from the trivialities of a night which comes upon Westminster when Piccadilly is gay.

This and Trafalgar Square in London are the two most impressive and well-balanced squares in Great Britain. Walter Scott is its Nelson skied on a great pillar with his plaid over the wrong shoulder and a lightning conductor sticking like a dart from the back of his neck. Here, among stone horsemen, are some of Glasgow's few trees.

I am amazed by the apparent size of Glasgow. Her million and a quarter people are squeezed into a lesser space than that occupied by several other great cities, and this compression gives a feeling of immensity. Here are miles of main streets, all wide, all marked by a certain grim and solid quality – shops as fine as any in Bond Street; clubs as reserved and Georgian as any in Pall Mall – and in a few yards you leave a street in which you could spend £1,000 on something for a woman's throat, to enter a street, equally broad and almost as well lit, in which perhaps the most expensive thing is a cut from the sheep whose corpse hangs head down, its horns in blood and sawdust ...

This meeting of extremes is characteristic of Glasgow. The splendour of riches and the abjectness of poverty, seen so close together, appear sharper than in most great cities.

This close-togetherness of Glasgow is one of its most important features. It means that a million and a quarter people live nearer the heart of their city than in any other social phenomenon of this size. This, I believe, explains Glasgow's clean-cut individuality. There is nothing half-hearted about Glasgow. It could not be any other city. And it is not a suburban city like London.

Glasgow plays the part of Chicago to Edinburgh's Boston. Glasgow is a city of the glad hand and the smack on the back; Edinburgh is a city of silence until birth or brains open the social circle. In Glasgow a man is innocent until he is found guilty; in Edinburgh a man is guilty until he is found innocent. Glasgow is willing to believe the best of an unknown quantity; Edinburgh, like all aristocracies, the worst!'

But the great difference between Scotland's two great cities is not a cultural versus a financial tradition. It is something deeper. Both these are poses. Edinburgh pretends to be more precious than she is; Glasgow pretends to be more material than she is. Hence the slight self-consciousness of the one and the slight roughness of the other. The real difference between these two cities is that Edinburgh is Scottish and Glasgow is cosmopolitan. That is why they will always secretly admire each other; also why Edinburgh is definitely the capital.

Glasgow is a mighty and an inspiring human story. She is Scotland's anchor to reality. Lacking her, Scotland would be a backward country lost in poetic memories and at enmity with an age in which she was playing no part. Glasgow, facing west to the new trade-ways of the world, rose after the Union, calling to Highlands and Lowlands to forget old scores and to take a hand in the building of that new world which was to begin on a Sabbath afternoon in the spring of 1765 when James Watt walked over Glasgow Green occupied with sinful week-day thoughts. The new age began sinfully on that Sabbath, for James Watt had solved the problem of the separate condenser; and as he walked over Glasgow Green a changed world lay pregnant in his brain: a world of steel and iron, tall chimneys and speed.

All over the world the last candles of the eighteenth century guttered and died. Glasgow rose: a Liverpool and a Manchester in one; a monument to the genius and the vigour of the Scot.

The Falls of Dochart, Perthshire

7
Galloway and
Dumfries

The name was McGuffog.

I saw it written up over a shop in a town. I made enquiries about what was, to me, an unknown clan; but no-one seemed to think it at all interesting or remarkable. In another town I saw over a shop an even less credible name – McHarrie.

These are good Galloway names. The meaning of Galloway is the 'Land of the Stranger Gaels'. It comes from Gall, a stranger, and Gaidhel, the Gaels; and it is interesting to find that these queer Macs, or stranger Gaels, still exist in great numbers in the local telephone directory.

Here is a short selection:

McClumpha	McHaffie
McCrindle	McKeand
McMeeking	McMiken
McSkimming	McCubbin
McCutcheon	McDavid
McFadzean	McWhirter
McQuaker	

These names, many of which suggest the queer Macs that occurred in Ireland during the Irishing of the Normans, go right back into Galloway history, and their owners are as justly proud of them as more normal clansmen. But until the visitor becomes accustomed to them, it seems as though some whimsical Barrie has been having a game with the shop fronts!

The Gallovidian has always been a mystery to the historian. He remained a Pict of Galloway when the Southern and the Northern Picts submerged their identity in an alliance with the Irish or the Scots. When Kenneth MacAlpine, king of the Dalriadic Scots, defeated the Picts

Buchan Falls, Glen Trool

with the help of the Danes in A.D. 844, he claimed all central Scotland as his kingdom, but Galloway remained outside it, the last stronghold of the mysterious Pict.

'The fremit (not a-kin) Scot o' Gallowa'' is a tag that has stuck to these people through history. The original charter of Melrose Abbey in 1144 is addressed to 'the Normans, English, Scots and Galwegians of the whole realm'. As recently as the sixteenth century Gaelic was spoken in Galloway.

The ancestry of the Galloway men is, therefore, a long and honoured one, and I creep through the little stone towns gazing with awe and respect at the names of the Strange Macs. Who knows what improbable things lie in the race memory of this people?

This is a strong country. So much has happened in it; and it wears the air of remembering everything.

In the Galloway heather the Roman outposts camped, gazing into the world's end, watching the Picts and longing to get back to rest billets in Carlisle. The Vikings beached their ships in the bays of Galloway, and to those shores came the Irish monks to clothe the land with Christ. There was a brief Golden Age, which is well remembered in Galloway, when a woman – Devorgilla, wife of John Balliol – left the world a love story under the broken arches of an abbey.

The Norman storm broke over Galloway until the air was darkened by the bowmen of Wales and Selkirk. The first Scots patriot, Wallace, plotted in Galloway. Men hunted Bruce through Galloway, and from Galloway he took the shaggy little horse that carried him at Bannockburn. After centuries of fighting, the hills of Galloway heard the chanting of psalms and saw the Covenanters assembling on the high moors – it is the greatest and the most solemn memory of this land – and so in time

every small kirkyard received its martyr.

Of the crowded memories of Galloway this is the strongest.

Not far off from the town of Castle Douglas, lying on a little island in the Dee, is a square keep of grey stones whose eight-foot-thick walls still bear the marks of cannonade and assault. This was the nest of those wild eagles – the Douglases – whose history is the history of Scotland. I went over to it and found it to be a mere shell. Its walls, from which men-at-arms watched the hills of Galloway, cease raggedly in mid-air, fret-worked against the sky.

Threave Castle was built by Archibald the Grim, the third earl of Douglas, who was the natural son of that mighty Douglas who fell at Otterburn in the light of the new moon, with three spears in his body and a battle-axe in his skull. Archibald the Grim, Lord of Galloway, first enters history in the sudden and unlikely way men did in his day – on the field of Poitiers! He was a dark and ugly lad and was known to his companions as 'Blac Archibalde'. But he wore a splendid suit of armour at Poitiers. He was captured by the English and escaped, thanks to the mental agility of a brother Scot – Sir William Ramsay of Colluthie. They were both prisoners. When Douglas was brought in, Ramsay pretended to fly into a violent passion:

'You treacherous hound,' he shouted, 'how dared you steal my cousin's armour? Cursed be the hour of your birth, for he sought you all day and for want of his armour was slain by an arrow in camp, as I myself saw. Come! Pull off my boots.'

As young Archibald, playing the part of a servant, knelt to pull off his compatriot's boots Sir William caught him a blow on the mouth, explaining to the disappointed English that the lad was not a great noble, as they believed, but a rogue and a scullion as they could tell from his face. As in fact Archibald had the reputation of being 'more like a coco (cook-boy) than a noble' the ruse worked well, and he was set free on the payment of a nominal ransom of forty shillings. This must have delighted every thrifty Scot within hearing, for had Douglas been recognised, his ransom would have been enormous!

In later life Archibald found himself Lord of Galloway 'because he took great trouble to purge the country of English blood'. It was assumed, no doubt, that if he could do this he might be capable of dealing with a district as fractious as Galloway! From this grey square tower in the river he administered the affairs of all lands between the Nith and the Cree.

His household was regal and his little island in the Dee housed an army that was the terror of the surrounding country. I noticed from the doorway a projecting stone and asked the man who had taken me to the island what it was.

' 'Tis the gallows knob,' he said. 'The Earl of Douglas used to boast that it never lacked a tassel.'

He mentioned a small mound on the west side of the loch which is supposed to have been the pit in which the skeletons were buried after they had rotted on the gallows knob.

The Galloway Kirk stands roofless among its dead, lost also in death. No bells have rung for centuries from the belfry where the wild birds nest; and the ivy clings to the old stones as if to save them from utter dissolution. The kirkyard, like most Scottish kirkyards, is a riot of lush grass. Briars fling their wild arms over headstones and climb the pedestals of memorial urns. The nobleman, lying in a walled place apart, sleeps beneath his coat-of-arms; and all around the worthy villagers lie beneath grey headstones that lean this way and that as if weary of waiting for the last trumpet. And there is no sound but the bees in the briar bushes and the softness of wood pigeons in the trees above.

In this acre of expended sorrow one stone alone looks as though men still remembered it. The grass around it is trampled by the feet of the curious. Those who visit this stone sometimes scrape away the green moss in order to read better the words engraved there, and give it an air of life in surroundings that tell only of death and forgetfulness. This stone says that the men who lie beneath it were 'hanged without law for adhering to the Word of God'. This happened in the 'killing time', when the Covenanters, fighting a war of conscience for fifty years, took the Lord's Supper in the heather of the Galloway muirs.

And the stranger who stands idly in these Galloway kirkyards, tries to force his mind backward through time in order to understand this religious war in which Scotsmen who abhorred Popery died like Catholic saints. The Englishman will think that, in spite of Smithfield and its faggots, the Reformation in England was a pale thing compared with Scotland's Reformation. The English made a funny song about the Vicar of Bray, who turned Protestant and then Catholic as it suited him. That song could never have been written or sung in Scotland. And it may seem to a man, as he stands over the graves of Scotsmen who were shot down for their faith, that one of the big differences between the two nations is this: compromise has always been the second nature of the English, while the Scots do not know the meaning of the word . . .

I was blown into Kirkcudbright in the dead of night by one of the most violent storms I have encountered in Scotland. The rain fell in sheets. The wind shuddered at windows and doors: it came sweeping round corners with the fury of an invading army.

I saw a town built for such gales: streets of low stone houses crouching in the fury of the night, the weary ruin of a castle, and a wide, muddy estuary at low tide, with the rain sweeping over it like blown smoke. The scene had the quality of one of those early bioscope travel pictures, taken apparently in perpetual rain and concluded in a sudden onset of liverish spots and sheet-lightning.

There was one building that made me stop, even in this storm. It was the old Tolbooth: a long Tudor building with a tower like that of a church. A flight of outside steps leads up to the door. Iron manacles, in which offenders were exhibited in the old days, hang from the walls. Seldom have I seen a more sinister building.

Cottages at Kirkcudbright

It is the sort of thing you see in unknown villages in the south of France. It looks as though it had walked into Scotland from the pages of Dumas. It suggests moss-troopers, hackbuteers, dubskelpers, and all manner of fly-by-nights.

There is one grand virtue in a stormy night. If you are late enough you are at once admitted to that snug little room which exists at the back of every Scottish hotel, where a vast fire is always burning and where a glass of special whisky waits for favoured guests.

The landlord was a young Scotsman who had fought in Gallipoli. We talked of Chocolate Hill and Suvia Bay and then, of course, we became local, and I was told the legend that Burns wrote 'Scots wha hae' in this hotel.

I took no sides in this contentious question. The same proud claim is put forward, I believe, by the Murray Arms Hotel at Gatehouse of Fleet, while a third tradition insists that Burns composed the greatest of all Scotland's national lyrics as he travelled in a thunderstorm across the moors near Lochanbreck, writing it out afterwards in the Bay Horse at Gatehouse, which is now demolished.

I went to bed in a high, windy room. The storm hurled itself at the windows. In the middle of the night three black ghosts entered and, lighting a candle, I discovered that three blinds were blowing in on me . . .

In the morning what a change: I looked out on an irreproachable Scottish town. There was a row of whitewashed houses, a milkman going his rounds, and at the end of the street was the Tolbooth, looking almost friendly in the morning sun.

The word Kirkcudbright, which looks so uncouth in print and is so soft in speech – Kir-coo-brie – was once spelt Kilcudbrit, a combination of two words *cil* and *Cudbert*, the church or cell of St. Cuthbert.

This place is one of the many in the Scottish Lowlands and in the north of England in which the monks of Lindisfarne, flying before the Danes, rested awhile with the bones, or rather the miraculously preserved body, of St. Cuthbert. Once a shepherd lad somewhere near Melrose, Cuthbert became one of the most revered saints in Britain. In the half century before the Norman Conquest Canute, in a mood of exuberant repentance, walked five miles barefoot to pray before Cuthbert's shrine at Durham. The capital of the Stewartry shared the sanctity which followed the incorruptible corpse of Cuthbert wherever it rested, but the Gallovidians celebrated their distinction in a singularly pagan manner, for we learn from the Abbot of Rievaulx that they were in the habit of tying a wretched bull to a stake and baiting it in honour of the saint. What an incredible time the early missionaries must have had in attempting to graft Christianity to the natural paganism of Man!

Dundrennan Abbey lifts its broken arches a few miles from the waters of Solway Firth. Old gravestones lie in the grass, bitten by the wind and rain, or stand up-ended against mossy walls with the faint figures of dead men carved on them. Dundrennan village, a single row of cottages, runs along a slight hill at the back of the Abbey, from which on clear days you can see, across twenty miles of water, the blue hills of Cumberland lying fold on fold. So near they seem on bright days that you can pick out white farms and little bright green fields.

You walk down a steep path and enter the ruins of the great church which Fergus, King of Galloway, erected to the glory of God in 1142. It was colonised by monks from Rievaulx in Yorkshire.

I think you should sit for a long time in that lovely chapter house, now open to the sky, and

remember the greatest memory of this abbey – the last night that Mary Stuart spent in Scotland.

Eleven days after young Willie Douglas stole the key of Lochleven Castle and rowed the Queen from eleven months of captivity, her nobles gathered round her to fight the Battle of Langside.

It is the unlucky morning of May 13, 1568. Mary, Queen of Scots, sitting on a palfrey, overlooks the village of Langside, a few miles from Glasgow. In three-quarters of an hour she is flying for her life. Her army is routed. Search parties are after her. She is guided by Lord Herries to the wilds of Galloway. She sees this bleak land for the second time, and she sees it through her tears.

The first day she rides sixty miles. As the horses are spent they are turned loose and the fugitives take to the heather. They move only by night. They hide in glens and caves. Mary's head is shaved and she wears a dark wig. When she passes over a bridge her followers destroy it; and so, painfully, the broken Queen comes out of the Galloway highlands to the soft country of the Solway shore.

A more hopeful race than the Stuarts never existed. Even as she flies like a gipsy over the mountains this young woman of twenty-six is full of new hopes. She will go to her cousin Elizabeth, and together they will make plans. Mary has always longed to meet Elizabeth. In failure and despair her heart has always turned to her successful cousin of England.

At Dundrennan the monks meet her. History says that she spent the last night in their abbey, but legend says that a lodging was found for her outside the abbey precincts. The story goes that the poor Queen, lonely, weary, and a prey to the horrors that continually afflicted her, ached for human companionship. Her women had scattered after the Battle of Langside. She had sent

them flying in different directions to puzzle her pursuers. Now she was alone with the night before her. She noticed a little boy, and asked that he might be allowed to sleep with her. So the Queen of Scots slept her last night in Scotland holding in her arms an unknown child.

Not far from the abbey, at a place called Port Mary, is a big stone washed by the tide. They say it was from this stone that in the morning the Queen embarked in a fishing boat for England.

Men kneel as the Queen of Scots says goodbye to Scotland. The Lord Abbot blesses her and the monks pray for her. She will come again with a victorious army from England!

Some hint of her fate, some foreknowledge of the nineteen years of captivity ahead of her, and of the block at Fotheringay, seems to have been given to the Archbishop of St. Andrews, who, as the boat is casting off, plunges waist-deep into the water and, seizing the gunwale with both hands, begs and implores the Queen to stay in Scotland.

But sails fill with wind. It is a wild day. They work against wind and tide for four hours, and then ahead of them are the blue mountains of Cumberland. And the Queen steps ashore . . .

In the gardens of a country house which run down to the Galloway coast a man talked to me of Devorgilla as if he had met her at dinner last week; also as if he had once been in love with her.

My friend talked about the stormy days of King Alan and John Balliol as if they were recent history. He was proud because the Galloway men were privileged to form the van in battle, and he delighted in the memory of a King of Galloway who threatened the King of Norway with a navy. But when he mentioned

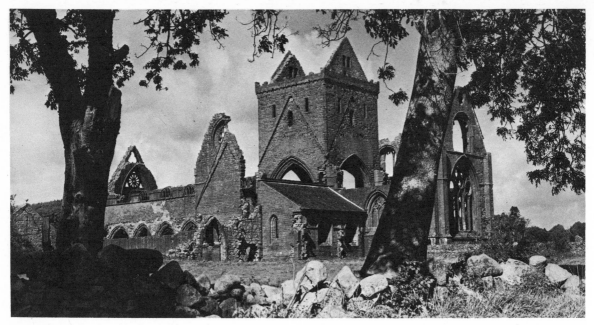

Devorgilla he used words and a voice which might have made his wife jealous.

'Devorgilla is still a lovely memory in Galloway,' he said, 'although she died over six centuries ago. And really, when you think of it, how few people are remembered only for their virtue and piety; how few widows for their fidelity! This long-dead lady has influenced all my life . . .'

I knew what he meant. He is a Balliol man; and Devorgilla – not her husband – is the real founder of Balliol College, Oxford.

When she died the monks made a grave for her before the high altar of Sweetheart Abbey. She died in an English shire. The funeral cortege came slowly northward into Galloway; and at last, to solemn chanting and in the light of tapers of unbleached wax, they placed her in the good earth of Galloway, which she loved above all other earth.

The Mull of Galloway is, in a sense, the Land's End of Scotland.

It is the extremity of a long slender strip about thirty miles in length that, but for the narrow neck of land between Glenluce and Stranraer, would be a little island off the coast of Wigtownshire. It has, like all out-of-the-way places, an island atmosphere. It reminds me very much of the Lleyn Peninsula in Wales.

I went there on a lovely windy morning, with the salt waters breaking over the splendid

Sands of Luce. I found myself in a soft, gentle land of woods and broad fields continually swept by sea winds. The Rhinns of Galloway, as this peninsula is termed, have a character of their own; and I imagine that ways of speech and habits, long vanished from what one thinks of as 'the mainland', are to be found here among the secluded little lanes and the lonely white farms.

The Mull itself is a small steep promontory whose tall cliffs drop sheer to the sea. I had no idea that such fine rock scenery was to be found at the Mull. There is a lighthouse on the point and the lighthouse-keeper, an Arran man, told me that on clear days he can see Ireland, the Isle of Man, the Cumberland hills, the Paps of Jura and the Merrick.

The Merrick is the highest hill in the south of Scotland, and is generally observed dozing in a white cloud like an old man asleep under a handkerchief. Sometimes, when he awakes with his head in the light of the sun, foolish people like myself think to outwit the old gentleman and so, grasping our sticks, we set off in his direction with great dispatch and vigour, but, lo, in the twinkling of an eye the Merrick whistles towards the Atlantic and up comes a cloud which he promptly assumes.

Even if you fail to climb the Merrick it is worth exploring the glorious five miles of Glen Trool. Where the road reaches its highest point is a magnificent view of the loch lying below, trees creeping down the flank of the opposite hills, little islands of tall dark firs near the shore, and on a piece of high ground overlooking Loch Trool an immense boulder poised upon a plinth.

The Bruce Monument is perfectly placed, for it was in this glen and on the surrounding hills that Bruce wandered as a fugitive, a lonely, hunted king without a kingdom, in the days after his famous episode with the spider, which is said to have occurred in a cave in Rachryne Isle.

Bruce had been hiding, first in Rachryne Isle and then in Arran, when he descended on the Galloway shores. He had his spies on the mainland, who had arranged that when the time was ripe a fire would be lit which the King would see from his cave on the east side of the island. It was early spring. The farmers were about to burn the heather. At the sight of the first blaze Bruce launched his galleys, believing it to be the signal. He landed in a grey March morning with three hundred wild and shaggy Highlanders. They were hungry and desperate. They raided a hamlet and then made for the hills. Bruce's plight was now desperate. He had landed by mistake in the one district in all Scotland which detested his cause: the land of Comyn and Balliol. Scots and English were closing round him. It would seem impossible that any man could escape from the hedge of steel that fenced him in the hills. The viceroy, Aymer de Valence, waited on the border of Ayrshire with 700 archers. The Nithsdale passes were watched by 70 horse and 200 archers. Sir Geoffrey de Moubray with three captains and a force of 300 men was sent to search the solitudes of Glen Trool. And through Ayrshire marched 800 Highlanders under John of Lorn.

It was from John of Lorn that Bruce made his most marvellous escape. This man had brought with him a bloodhound that had belonged to Bruce and was devoted to his master. He let the dog loose on the hills. The chase became so hot that Bruce and a companion were actually seen. Five Highlanders were told off to run after them and slay them. Three attacked Bruce and two his companion. The five Highlanders were slain and, with the main body almost in sight, the fugitives sped exhausted over the crags, coming at length to a stream through a wood. They travelled in the water for some time and, crossing to the other bank, destroyed the scent.

Near the stately little town of Ayr, and not far from the Brig o' Doon, stands an old clay biggin' against the road. Here Burns was born in 1759. This cottage, with its low, white walls and its close-cropped thatch, can be compared as a place of worship with the Birthplace, Stratford-on-Avon, but Burns means more to Scotland than Shakespeare means to England. Shakespeare is reverenced in England; in Scotland Burns is loved.

He interpreted Scotland to herself, whereas Scott interpreted Scotland to outsiders. Everyone in Scotland has grown up with Burns; many quote him who have never read a line of him, because his songs are in the air, his verses are something heard round the fireside; and it is never possible to tell when a man of humble birth and education quotes the poet whether he is quoting from the printed page or merely remembering something which he has known all his life. There is no English poet whose songs have curled up like an old dog on the hearthstone. England has no bard.

Burns was the Pan of Scotland. (I believe Henley thought of this before I was born.) He pricked his ears to every lusty paganism. He was a natural reaction to Calvinism.

Centuries of repression spoke in him; he was Scotland's only great expression of animal

humanity since the Reformation. He snapped his pagan fingers at the gloomy, kirk-made, ugly, vindictive, narrow-minded, key-hole-gazing tradesman's god and opened his arms to the beauty of the earth. He was a faun born in an age of elastic-sided boots. He sinned and he sinned again, yet now and again there shot through him – for so strong is heredity – a twinge of respect for the ethics of gloom. More than once his wenching must have been interrupted by a faint prophetic smell of brimstone.

He was a peasant who had to bear the pain of voicing the inarticulateness of centuries of peasants. In his voice, clear and unhesitant, one heard all the joys and sorrows which lay unspoken for generations in the hearts of men who work with their hands. This great silence he broke magnificently. He sang in thirty-six years all the things that men like him in every other particular but that of expression had failed to sing for centuries. No wonder he died young. It was a great strain on the throat.

The Burns enthusiast is happy among the world's literary pilgrims. If you go in search of Shakespeare you walk in a half light. With Burns, however, you walk in no half light but in the full glare of topographical facts. Ayrshire and Dumfriesshire are studded with that which booksellers call by the dreadful name of 'Burnsiana'. When you tire of visiting buildings hallowed by contact with the bard, you can go round placing flowers on the tombs of his characters. Never has poet left so many visiting places for posterity.

Burnsiana begins at Kilmarnock. Here his first volume of poems were issued by John Wilson in 1786. The Low Church in this town (rebuilt since the poet's day) was the church of the poem 'The Ordination', and the Angel Hotel in Kilmarnock is mentioned in that poem as 'Begbie's'. In the churchyard is an epitaph by Burns on Tam Samson. In Kay Park is a Burns

Memorial and a museum in which they show you the poet's draught-board.

We come to Ayr. Here is the Tam o' Shanter Inn. There are the Auld Brig and the New Bridge. At Alloway is the birthplace and the museum and the Burns Monument, the beautiful curved Brig o' Doon, and the 'auld haunted kirk'. In the kirkyard of Kirkoswald are the graves of Tam o' Shanter and Souter Johnnie. The real name of the first was Douglas Graham and of the second John Davidson. They enjoy together the strangest of all immortality, rather like that of the fly in the amber: the fame of having blundered into the orbit of genius.

Ayr shares the glory of the poet's birth; Dumfries that of his unhappy death. Here is his house and his tomb. There are two taverns in which undoubtedly he drank: the Globe and the Hole in the Wa'. A few miles from Dumfries is Lincluden. Burns here saw his 'Vision of Libertie'. Here also is the farm, Ellisland, where the poet worked and wrote. He composed 'Mary in Heaven' here.

This is just a brief summary. I have no doubt that a zealous Burns pilgrim could wear his boots out in a conscientious endeavour to visit every bank, brae, burn and howff associated with the poet in the counties of Ayr and Dumfries. Compared with the topographical ubiquity of Burns, Wordsworth in Lakeland seems like a lodger.

It was dark when I went through the streets of Dumfries to look at the old bridge. I think this must be the oldest bridge in Scotland. It was built by the widowed Queen Devorgilla who established Balliol College, Oxford, as a students' hostel at some time in the thirteenth century. What queer links there are between towns in an ancient country!

The dark waters passed through the six arches, and a little way off, at a different angle, the new bridge crossed the Nith. It is curious that all three rivers associated with Burns—Ayr, Doon, and Nith – possess an old and a new bridge side by side.

I walked back through the cattle market to the High Street, and there I found the Globe Inn. They say – but I do not believe there is documentary evidence – that Burns after a carousal in the Globe collapsed on a step in the snow and caught a chill which hastened his end.

The inn is a kind of temple to the conviviality of Burns. Drinkers, like the vestal virgins, have kept alight an alcoholic enthusiasm in the bar for generations. After I had done my bit according to the custom, I felt rather lonely, standing there in the street with a late bus revving up to take the road to Ayr.

It was my last night in Scotland.

There was a lit window in the dark High Street. There was a burst of laughter, the warm laughter of friends saying good night. Then – how often have I heard it from Edinburgh to Aberdeen, from Inverness to Glasgow? – that national anthem which gathers into itself all the sweetness and the friendliness of this dear country:

> *Should auld acquaintance be forgot,*
>   *And never brought to min'?*
> *Should auld acquaintance be forgot,*
>   *And auld lang syne?*
>
> *For auld lang syne, my dear,*
>   *For auld lang syne.*
> *We'll tak' a cup o' kindness yet,*
>   *For auld lang syne . . .*

There was a burst of laughter, a whoop or two, and a volley of good nights.

Then silence . . .

In that silence a stranger said good-bye to Scotland.

Acknowledgments

For photographic permissions, acknowledgment is made to the following:
Peter Baker: page 52, 100, 124, 133, 138 lower, 151
J. Allan Cash: 11, 38, 39, 43, 44, 46, 50, 54, 57, 58, 66, 69, 70, 78, 80, 81, 82, 88, 110, 126, 128, 141, 142
A. F. Kersting: 8, 30, 36, 37, 41, 49, 120, 129, 134, 144
Eric Meadows: 20, 53, 87, 98, 101, 102
W. A. Sharp: 105
Tom Weir: 89 upper, 90, 91, 108, 113, 117
John Woolverton: 56, 60, 61, 62, 64, 65, 68, 72, 74, 84, 95
Aerofilms: 156
British Tourist Authority: 6, 12, 14, 16, 18, 22, 25, 28, 34, 76, 93, 96, 106, 114, 118, 122, 130, 135, 138 upper, 139, 140, 146, 154, 159
Her Britannic Majesty's Stationery Office: 24, 26, 32, 149, 153
National Monuments Record of Scotland: 33, 148
The Scotsman: 158
Scottish Tourist Board: 94

H. V. Morton's books on Britain

In Search of England   (1927)
The Call of England   (1928)
In Search of Scotland   (1929)
In Search of Ireland   (1930)
In Search of Wales   (1932)
In Scotland Again   (1933)
Ghosts of London   (1939)
H. V. Morton's London   (1940)
   (a trilogy of earlier books)
I Saw Two Englands   (1942)
In Search of London   (1951)
H. V. Morton's England   (1975)
   (a trilogy of earlier books)